J. H. Tenney

Sparkling and Bright

a new collection of hymns and tunes

J. H. Tenney

Sparkling and Bright
a new collection of hymns and tunes

ISBN/EAN: 9783337089825

Printed in Europe, USA, Canada, Australia, Japan

Cover: Foto ©Lupo / pixelio.de

More available books at **www.hansebooks.com**

SPARKLING ∴ ∴
∴ ∴ and BRIGHT.

A NEW COLLECTION OF

HYMNS AND TUNES

FOR

Sunday Schools, Young People's Societies of Christian Endeavor and all meetings for praise and worship.

BY
J. H. TENNEY and CHAS. EDW. PRIOR.

THE S. BRAINARD'S SONS CO.,
CHICAGO.

PREFACE

THE continued and increasing demand for new music for Sunday Schools and for Young People's Societies of Christian Endeavor has prompted us to prepare a new collection of hymns and tunes that would be adapted to the musical wants of both of these branches of Christian work. The aim and work of both of these great auxiliaries of the Christian Churches of America are so inter-connected that a book prepared for one should be suited to the needs of the other. With this fact in view the hymns and tunes of "SPARKLING AND BRIGHT" have been collected, arranged and edited, and are now offered to the public, in the belief that they will be found useful in the work of Christ, our beloved Master and Saviour, and with the prayer and in the hope that they will be blessed to the salvation of many souls, and to the glory of His name.

J. H. TENNEY.
CHAS. EDW. PRIOR.

INDEX OF SUBJECTS.

CHRISTIAN ENDEAVOR SONGS.—Nos. 4-10-12-14-21-22-23-25-31-36-37-39-41-47-54-56-59-65-66-67-73-74-77-78-82-83-84-89-94-102-107-112-125-126-128-130-144-150-151.

CHRISTIAN EXPERIENCE.—15-20-25-57-73-77-78-79-80-81-90-103-119-122-134.

FAITH AND TRUST.—5-8-18-21-25-30-33-41-70-80-81-87-92-95-98-111.

INVITATION.—26-29-37-38-50-52-55-60-85-91-108-111-117-118-133.

JESUS EXTOLLED.—6-13-15-16-19-54-94-109-119-127-147.

PRAYER.—32-42-44-64-88-104-125.

PRAISE.—3-27-40-51-53-84-93-97-109.

PENITENCE.—88-98-121-123.

ATONEMENT.—16-43-79-92-110-120.

HEAVEN.—11-19-35-45-49-61-62-63-96-99-124-129.

CHRISTMAS.—17-138-139-140-141-142.

EASTER.—58-69-143-145-146.

CHILDREN'S DAY.—58-68-69-72.

KING'S DAUGHTERS.—75-76-78-107-113-126.

INFANT CLASS.—18-42-46-64-70-74-85-86-100-105-131.

TEMPERANCE.—54-56-112-132-136.

OPENING AND CLOSING WORSHIP.—1-2-51-71-97-104-106-109.

Copyright MDCCCXC. by THE S. BRAINARD'S SONS Co.

Sparkling and Bright.

The Life of Jesus. Concluded.

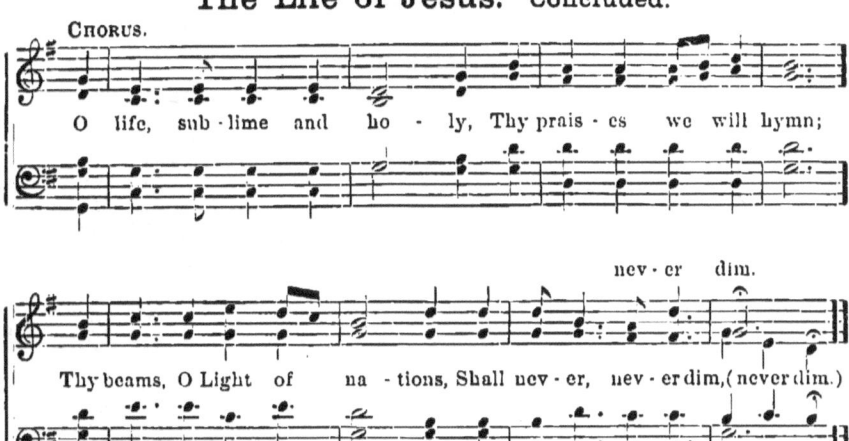

No. 7. Dear Saviour, Bend Thine Ear.

IDA L. REED. CHAS. EDW. PRIOR.

1. Dear Saviour, bend Thine ear, In tender mercy sweet;
   My humble pray'r to hear While kneeling at Thy feet.
2. Teach me to trust in thee, Forgive mine ev'ry sin,
   Dear Lord, I fain would be From ev'ry evil clean.
3. Let all my deeds be pure, All for thy holy name,
   May I for Thee endure, Each sorrow, care and pain.
4. Dear Saviour, fit my soul For mansions fair above,
   And then on heaven's shore Crown me with Thy fond love.

The Bells of the Beautiful City. Concluded.

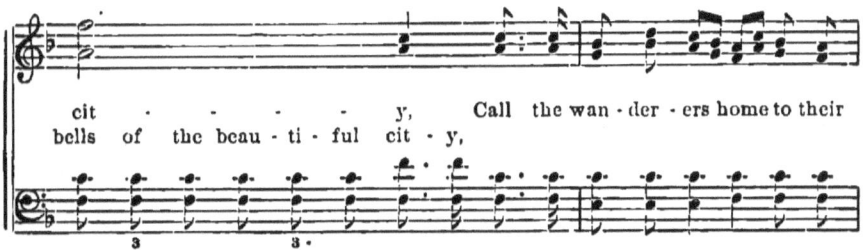

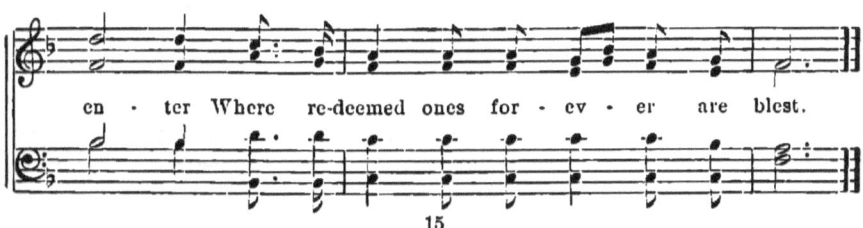

Shine Around Me. Concluded.

Just and ho-ly make me ev-er, Shine around me with the beautiful light of God.

No. 13. Rest of the Weary.

MONSELL. CHAS. EDW. PRIOR.

1. Rest of the wea - ry, Joy to the sad, Hope of the drea - ry, Light of the glad; Home of the stran - ger, Strength to the end, Ref - uge from dan - ger, Sav - iour and Friend.

2. When my feet stum - ble, To Thee I'll cry, Crown of the hum - ble, Cross of the high, When my steps wan - der, O - ver me bend, Tru - er and fond - er, Sav - iour and Friend.

3. Ev - er con - fess - ing Thee, I will raise Un - to Thee bless - ing, Glo - ry and praise; All my en - deav - or, World with-out end, Thine to be ev - er, Sav - iour and Friend.

17

No. 14. Be of Good Cheer.

E. A. BARNES. CHAS. EDW. PRIOR.

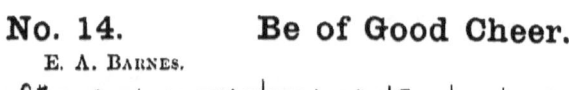

1. The ves-sel is out in the tem-pest, The sail-ors are in dis-may;
2. The sail-ors are los-ing their cour-age, And dark-ness is o-ver all;
3. The sail-ors in trou-ble and dan-ger, Are breast-ing the wind and wave;
4. And sure-ly in dan-ger or sor-row, The mes-sage is sweet to-day;

When a form is seen on the bil-lows, And Je-sus is heard to say,......
But a friend ap-pears in the tem-pest, And Je-sus is heard to call,......
When a voice comes o-ver the wa-ters, And Je-sus is near to save......
As in faith, we look to the Sav-iour, And lis-ten to hear Him say,......

CHORUS. (Matt. 14: 27.)

"Be of good cheer, be of good cheer, It is I, be not a-fraid;......
"Be of good cheer, O be of good cheer, It is I, it is I, be not a-fraid;

O be of good cheer, be of good cheer, It is I, be not a-fraid."
Be of good cheer, O be of good cheer,

No. 16. Who is This that Cometh?

Isa. 63: 1.

ELLEN C. WEBSTER. J. H. TENNEY.

1. Who is this that cometh from the land of E-dom?
   All His garments dyed in precious crimson blood?
   In the greatness of His strength we see Him trav'ling,
   We behold Him as the Mighty Son of God.

2. Who is this that cometh, with a heart of pity?
   In His hands a pardon for the wretched, poor?
   In His heart a blessing for the weak and wounded,
   For the tempted spirit, for the sick and sore.

3. Who is this that cometh to the wine-press lonely?
   Suff'ring on the cruel cross for all His own,
   Rising King and Conq'ror o'er His foes so mighty,
   Reigning now in glory on His shining throne.

Who is This that Cometh? Concluded.

Beautiful Bethlehem! Concluded.

No. 18. My Saviour Dear, I Come to Thee.

Rev. W. F. Cosner. Chas. Edw. Prior.

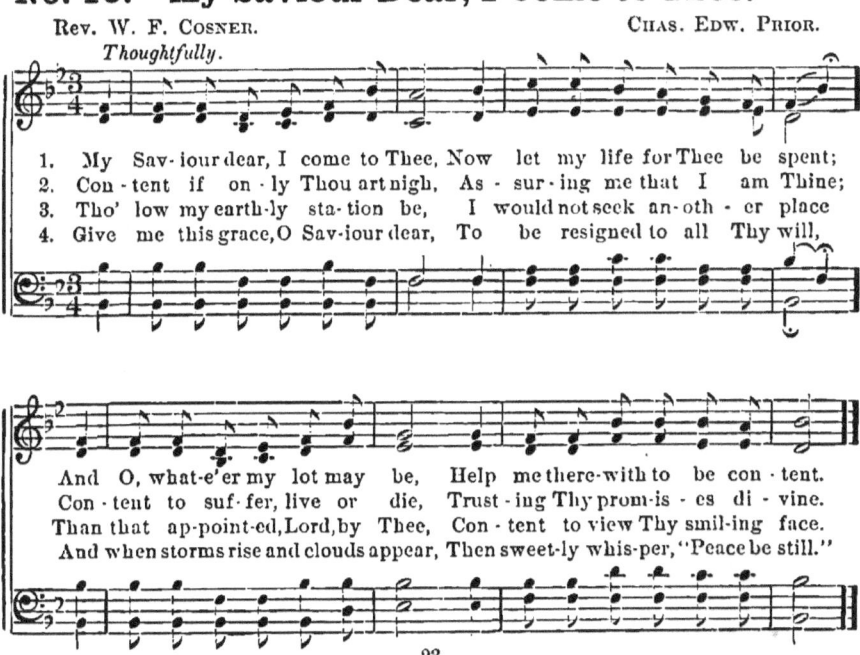

1. My Saviour dear, I come to Thee, Now let my life for Thee be spent;
2. Content if only Thou art nigh, Assuring me that I am Thine;
3. Tho' low my earthly station be, I would not seek another place
4. Give me this grace, O Saviour dear, To be resigned to all Thy will,

And O, what-e'er my lot may be, Help me therewith to be content.
Content to suffer, live or die, Trusting Thy promises divine.
Than that appointed, Lord, by Thee, Content to view Thy smiling face.
And when storms rise and clouds appear, Then sweetly whisper, "Peace be still."

Heaven shall Ring. Concluded.

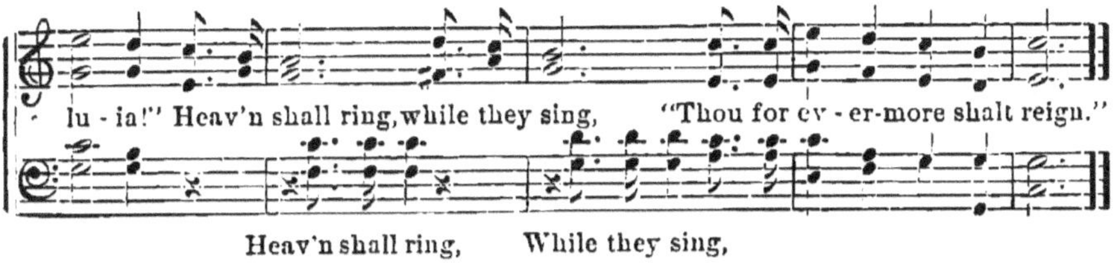

No. 20. I shall be Satisfied.

Dr. H. Bonar.
Moderato.
Rev. T. C. Neal.

1. When I shall wake in that fair morn of morns, After whose dawning nev-er night re-turns, And with whose glo-ry day e-ter-nal burns,
2. When I shall see Thy glo-ry face to face, When in Thine arms Thou wilt Thy child em-brace, When Thou shalt o-pen all Thy stores of grace,
3. When I shall meet with those that I have loved, Clasp in my ea-ger arms the long re-moved, And find how faith-ful Thou to me hast proved,
4. When I shall gaze up-on the face of Him Who for me died, with eye no lon-ger dim, And praise Him with the ev-er-last-ing hymn,

CHORUS.

I shall be sat-is-fied. I shall be sat-is-fied, I shall be sat-is-fied, I shall be sat-is-fied, By and by.

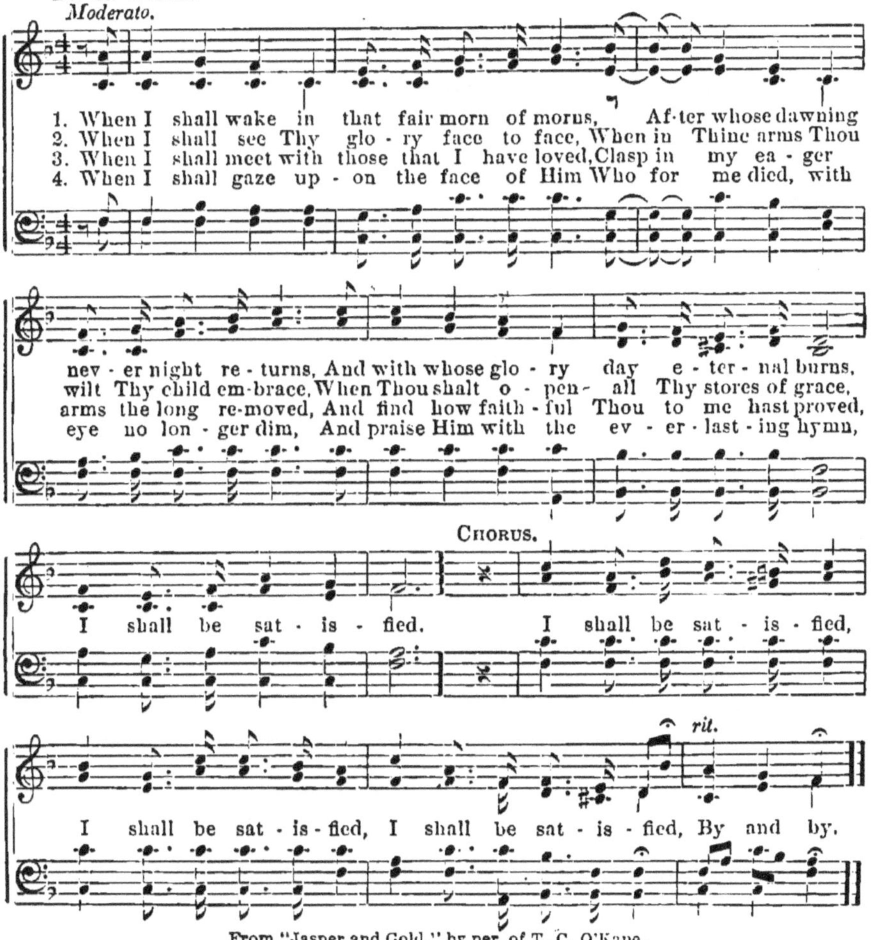

From "Jasper and Gold," by per. of T. C. O'Kane.

No. 21. Trust and Obey.

Rev. J. H. Sammis. D. B. Towner.

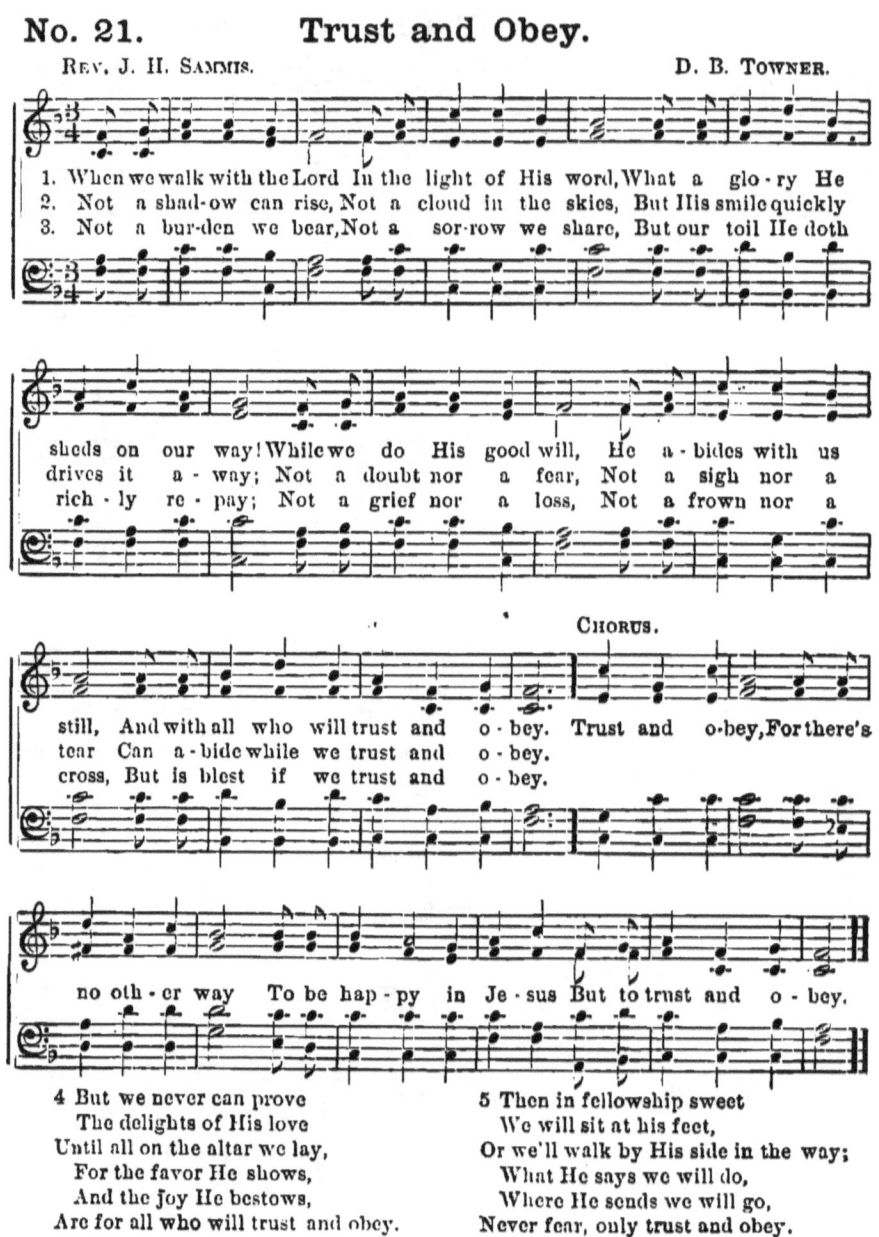

1. When we walk with the Lord In the light of His word, What a glo-ry He sheds on our way! While we do His good will, He a-bides with us still, And with all who will trust and o-bey.
2. Not a shad-ow can rise, Not a cloud in the skies, But His smile quickly drives it a-way; Not a doubt nor a fear, Not a sigh nor a tear Can a-bide while we trust and o-bey.
3. Not a bur-den we bear, Not a sor-row we share, But our toil He doth rich-ly re-pay; Not a grief nor a loss, Not a frown nor a cross, But is blest if we trust and o-bey.

CHORUS.
Trust and o-bey, For there's no oth-er way To be hap-py in Je-sus But to trust and o-bey.

4 But we never can prove
 The delights of His love
Until all on the altar we lay,
 For the favor He shows,
 And the joy He bestows,
Are for all who will trust and obey.

5 Then in fellowship sweet
 We will sit at his feet,
Or we'll walk by His side in the way;
 What He says we will do,
 Where He sends we will go,
Never fear, only trust and obey.

Copyright, 1887, by D. B. Towner. Used by per.

No. 23. On the Jericho Road.

Dr. J. J. Maxfield. W. A. Ogden.

1. On the Jer-i-cho road there is ser-vice to-day, For all who are read-y to work or to pray; A-round us are ly-ing the wound-ed and dy-ing, And few the Sa-mar-i-tans pass-ing that way.
2. On the Jer-i-cho road you will find him to-day, Your broth-er who wan-ders from Je-sus a-way; Oh, wait not to-mor-row, his deep cup of sor-row Is brim-ming and bit-ter, no lon-ger de-lay.
3. On the Jer-i-cho road man-y forc-es com-bine, To sti-fle the voice of the Spir-it Di-vine; A-bout us are ly-ing the wound-ed and dy-ing, Go, broth-er, and pour in the oil and the wine.

Chorus.

By per. of the Author.   28

On the Jericho Road. Concluded.

Jer-i-cho road, lead-ing down, (down, down, down,) The Le-vite goes care-less-ly by, Yet man-y who jour-ney a-long that way Are wounded and read-y to die.

No. 24. Sweet Thoughts of God.

R. N. Turner. W. F. Sherwin.

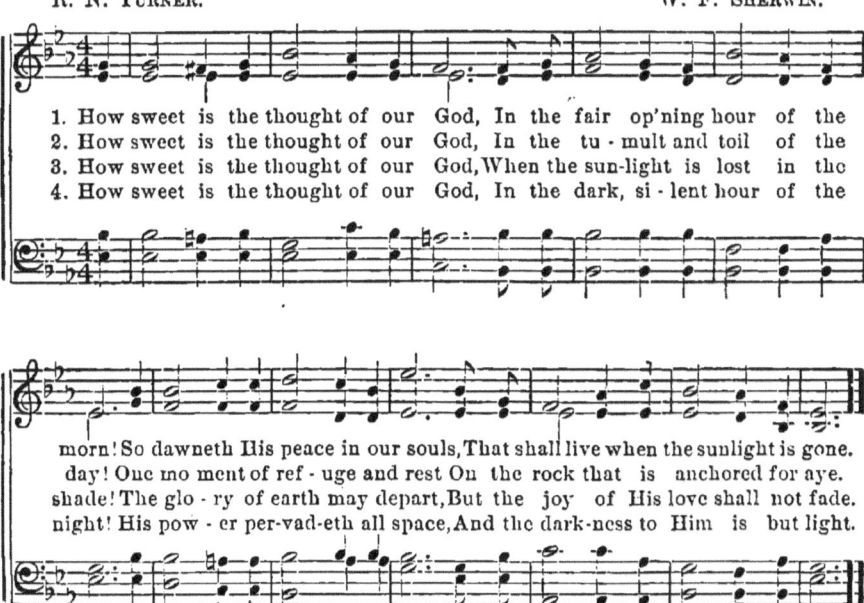

1. How sweet is the thought of our God, In the fair op'ning hour of the morn! So dawneth His peace in our souls, That shall live when the sunlight is gone.
2. How sweet is the thought of our God, In the tu-mult and toil of the day! One mo-ment of ref-uge and rest On the rock that is anchored for aye.
3. How sweet is the thought of our God, When the sun-light is lost in the shade! The glo-ry of earth may depart, But the joy of His love shall not fade.
4. How sweet is the thought of our God, In the dark, si-lent hour of the night! His pow-er per-vad-eth all space, And the dark-ness to Him is but light.

No. 27. The Bells of Heaven are Ringing.

"I say unto you, that likewise joy shall be in heaven over one sinner that repenteth." Luke xv: 7.

E. A. HOFFMAN. J. H. TENNEY.

1. Down at the feet of the low-ly Naz-a-rene, A pen-i-tent sin-ner in ear-nest pray'r is seen; The an-gels of heav-en be-hold the hallowed scene, And sing in re-joic-ing o'er sin-ners com-ing home.
2. Up at the gates of the bright and bet-ter land, There, ea-ger-ly wait-ing, the shin-ing ser-aphs stand To tell the glad tid-ings un-to the an-gel band, Of pen-i-tent sin-ners to Je-sus com-ing home.
3. Sweet 'tis to know that the voice of whis-pered pray'r As-cends up to heav-en up-on the balm-y air, And wakes 'mid the an-gels that throng the al-tar there, A thrill of re-joic-ing o'er sin-ners com-ing home.

CHORUS.

The bells of heav'n are ring-ing, The an-gel-hosts are sing-ing, The heav-ens thrill with praise,...... As choirs u-ni-ted raise...... A
The heav-ens thrill with praise,...... As choirs u-ni-ted

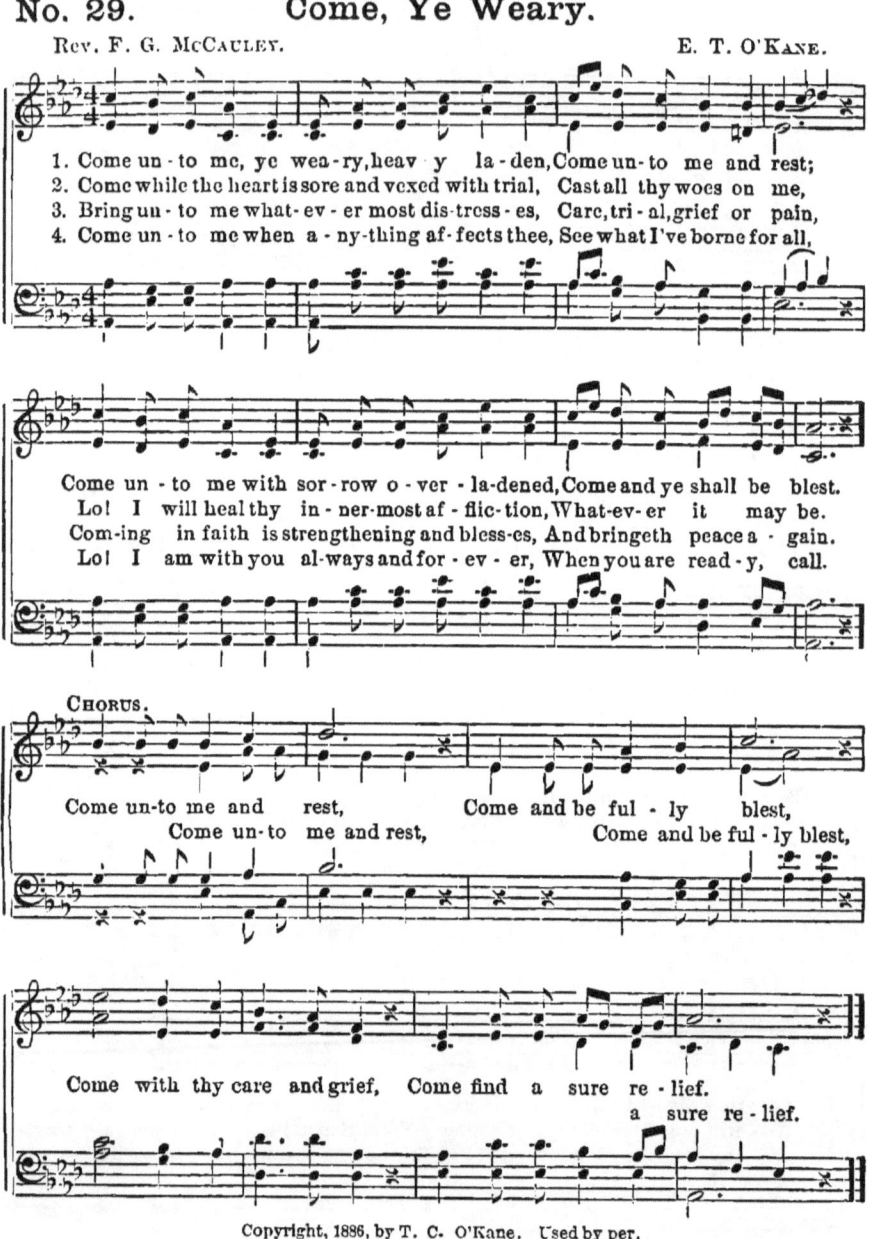

No. 31. How Shall I Live?

"Let your light so shine before men, that they may see your good works, and glorify your Father which is in heaven." Matt. v: 16.

Rev. C. W. Ray, D. D.   Chas. Edw. Prior.

1. How shall I live that my life may be tell-ing My faith and my trust in the Sav-iour Di-vine? How shall I live that a glory-crown'd dwell-ing, And snow-y white robe shall in heav-en be mine?
2. How shall I live that the heart of my Sav-iour Shall ev-er re-joice o'er the grace He has giv'n? How shall I live that my dai-ly be-hav-ior Shall wit-ness to men my as-sur-ance of heav'n?
3. How shall I live that the an-gels most ho-ly Shall gath-er a-round me when I come to die? How shall I live while so help-less and low-ly, That they with re-joic-ings shall bear me on high?
4. How shall I live that the ran-somed in glo-ry Will watch for my com-ing and meet me a-bove? How shall I live that the Sa-viour will own me, And bid me sit down to the feast of His love?

Chorus.

How shall I live? How shall I live? Blame-less-ly ev-er, How shall I live? How shall I live? Blamelessly

By permission.

How Shall I Live? Concluded.

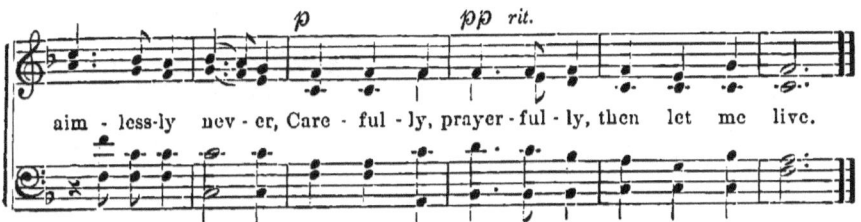

aim-less-ly nev-er, Care-ful-ly, prayer-ful-ly, then let me live.

No. 32. Thy Will be Done.

Rev. A. A. Haskins.   W. Irving Hartshorn. By per.

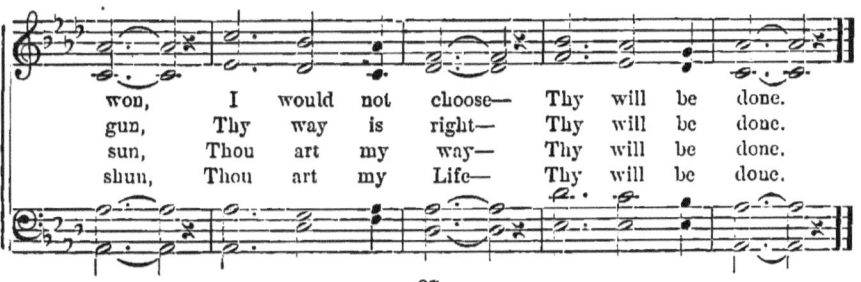

1. Not will of mine, O Ho-ly One, Fa-ther Di-vine,
2. Weak and dis-tress'd, Life's path I run, Thou know-est best,—
3. In pain and woe, With pleas-ures none, If Thou guide so,
4. Hopes of my youth Fade one by one, Thou art my Truth,

Thy will be done: To keep or lose Life's treas-ures
Thy will be done. Tho' sor-row's night, Quench joys be-
Thy will be done: With-out one ray Of star or
Thy will be done: Death's mor-tal strife I would not

won, I would not choose— Thy will be done.
gun, Thy way is right— Thy will be done.
sun, Thou art my way— Thy will be done.
shun, Thou art my Life— Thy will be done.

No. 33. Wait a Little, You May See!

E. R. Latta. Chas. Edw. Prior.

1. If be-set by doubts and fears, And no ray of light ap-pears,
2. If your hopes that seemed so bright, All are doomed to suf-fer blight,
3. Where there is no care and pain, It may all be ren-dered plain,

Wait a lit-tle, wait a lit-tle, you may see! If your
Wait a lit-tle, wait a lit-tle, you may see! What your
Wait a lit-tle, wait a lit-tle, you may see! Trust the

bur-den seems so great, That you scarce can bear the weight,
heart would fain pos-sess, Might bring on-ly wretch-ed-ness,
Lord and do the right, Till your faith shall turn to sight,

Wait a lit-tle, wait a lit-tle, you may see.

Wait a Little, You May See! Concluded.

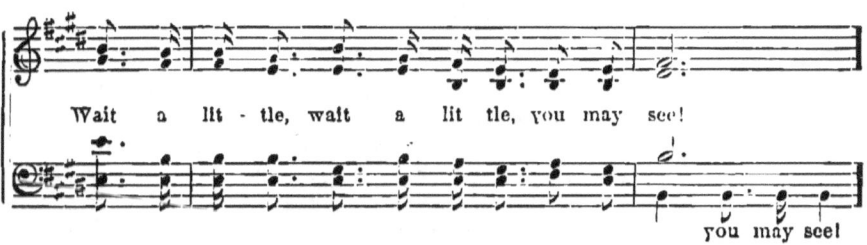

Tenting toward the Highlands. Concluded.

No. 36. Endure to the End

James 1: 12.

Mrs. E. C. Ellsworth.
J. H. Tenney.

1. Tho' fierce the temptation That bear-eth thee down, O yield not the strug-gle!
2. Tho' le-gions be-set thee, Shrink not in de-spair, While wag-ing the bat-tle,
3. When weak and discouraged, And read-y to faint, The great heart of Je-sus

O lose not thy crown! Thy Sav-iour hath promised, He sure will de-fend;
The Lord will be there; Thy foes may be man-y, God's arm will de-fend;
Wilt hear thy com-plaint; He'll give thee new cour-age, His help He will send,

Chorus.

By grace thou shalt conquer, En-dure to the end. A crown shall reward thee,
There's more that be for thee, En-dure to the end.
And thou shalt yet con-quer, En-dure to the end.

A king thou shalt be! Then up, for the vic-t'ry Is sure-ly with thee!

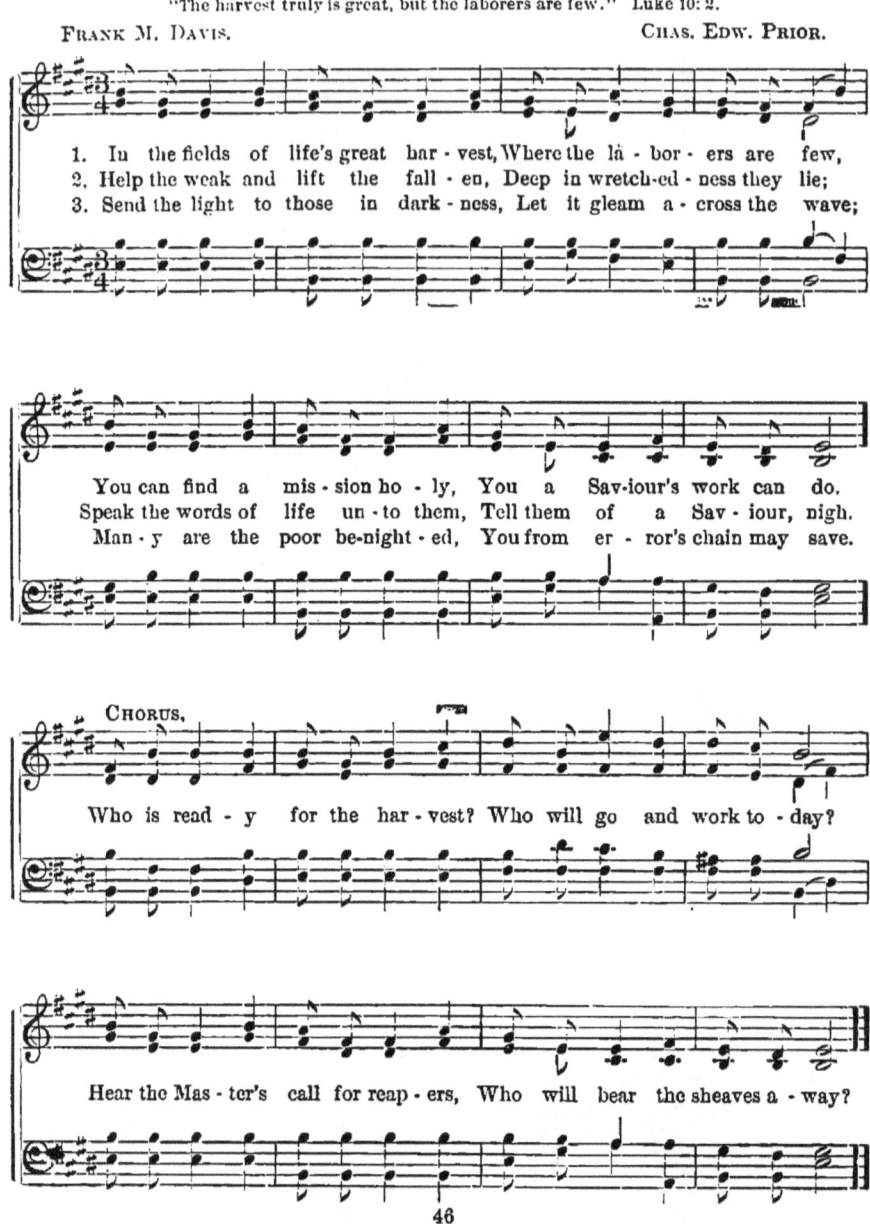

I Will Trust my Dear Redeemer. Concluded.

Him On the fair,............ e - ter - nal shore............
meet Him On the fair, e - ter - nal shore, Up-on the fair, e - ter-nal shore.

No. 42.   **Guide and Guard.**
"I will guide thee." Ps. 32: 8.

WHISPER SONG.   W. A. OGDEN.

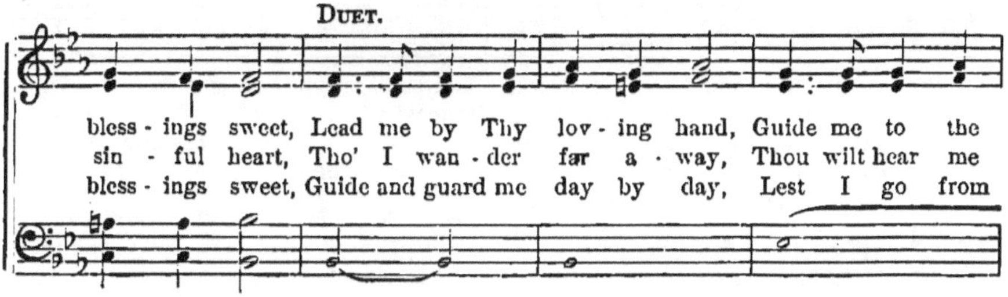

1. Bless - ed Je - sus, guide my feet, Fill me with Thy
2. Bless - ed Je - sus, take my heart, Take, O take my
3. Bless - ed Je - sus, guide my feet, Fill me with Thy

DUET.

bless - ings sweet, Lead me by Thy lov - ing hand, Guide me to the
sin - ful heart, Tho' I wan - der far a - way, Thou wilt hear me
bless - ings sweet, Guide and guard me day by day, Lest I go from

ALL.

bet - ter land, Guide me, guide me, Guide and guard Thy child.
as I pray, Help me, help me, Guide and guard Thy child.
Thee a - stray, Guide me, guide me, Guide and guard Thy child.

Copyright, 1885, by W. A. Ogden. Used by per.

Through the Blood of Jesus. Concluded.

CHORUS.

Pre-cious blood! crim-son flood! Oh, the pre-cious blood of Je-sus! Hal-le-lu-jah, we shall gain a glo-rious crown, Thro' the precious blood of Je-sus!

No. 44. Remember Me.

"Remember me, O Lord, with the favor that thou bearest unto thy people." Ps.—106:4.

J. H. TENNEY.

1. When storms a-round are sweep-ing, O Lord, re-mem-ber me.
2. When walk-ing on life's o-cean O Lord, re-mem-ber me.
3. When weight of sin op-press-es, O Lord, re-mem-ber me.
4. All thro' the life that's mor-tal, O Lord, re-mem-ber me.

When lone my watch I'm keep-ing, O Lord, re-mem-ber me.
Con-trol its rag-ing mo-tion, O Lord, re-mem-ber me.
When dark de-spair dis-tress-es, O Lord, re-mem-ber me.
And when I pass death's por-tal, O Lord, re-mem-ber me.

Re-mem-ber me, re-member me, O Lord, re-member me, Lord, remember me.

Living for Jesus. Concluded.

do,............ Thus would I ev - er my jour - ney pur - sue.
all that I do,

No. 48. Rest, Weary One.

MARIA STRAUB.   J. H. TENNEY.

1. Rest, dear - est { broth - er, / sis - ter, / one, for } thy jour - ney is o'er, Rest, sweet - ly rest, on the beau - ti - ful shore; Safe - ly at last thou hast reached the bright goal, Fa - - ther-land, home of the soul.

Land of our Fa-ther, the home of the soul.

2 Never again shall thy storm beaten breast,
Sigh, deeply sigh, for the sweet "land of rest;"
Gone to the Saviour's bright mansion a-bove,
Rest (ever rest) in the light of His love.

3 Rest, dearest { brother, / sister, / one, for } thy journey is [o'er,
Rest, sweetly rest, on the beautiful shore;
Dangers and troubles shall harm thee no more,
Rest (sweetly rest) on the beautiful shore.

From "Songs of the Cross;" by per

Calling Again. Concluded.

lan-guished for thee, Wea-ry one, dy-ing one, come un-to me."

No. 56.　　O, Look Not Back!

Mrs. E. C. Ellsworth.　　Phil. 3: 13, 14.　　Arr. from Mozart.

1. O, look not back in all thy race, Temp-ta-tion fol-lows near;
2. O, look not back! it mat-ters naught, Tho' far thy steps have come,
3. O, look not back, but on-ward press; The mo-ments quick-ly fly;
4. O, look not back! for yon-der waits A glad, a sweet sur-prise;

O, look not back, but on-ward press, The goal must soon ap-pear.
If, fail-ing now, thy wea-ry feet Shall nev-er reach thy home.
Thy time re-deem, the wan-ing day In haste is pass-ing by.
Thy fly-ing feet shall reach the goal; Thy hand shall grasp the prize.

Chorus.

Then haste thee on! press on! press on! A-way, and thou shalt win!

O, stay not in thy heav'n-bound course, If thou wouldst en-ter in.

No. 57. We Shall Rest.

Dr. C. Nysewander. J. R. Bryant.

1. We shall rest when life's last strug-gle On the plains of time is o'er;
2. We shall rest, but now we're toil-ers, Har-vest-ing the gold-en grain;
3. We shall rest in heav-en's ar-bors, Naught shall ev-er mar our peace;

We shall rest from care and la-bor, When we reach that gold-en shore.
We shall rest, but not till Je-sus Bids us from our work re-frain.
We shall rest, but rest in heav-en, Is re-joic-ing, sing-ing praise.

Chorus.

We shall rest, we shall rest, We shall rest from care and la-bor,

We shall rest, we shall rest, When life's har-vest-time is o'er.

No. 58. Hail the Mighty Conqueror!

(For Easter and Children's Day.)

Mrs. E. W. Chapman.   J. H. Tenney.

1. Bright-est flow'rs and lil-ies sweet, Lay we now at Je-sus' feet;
2. When night's sa-ble wing had gone, An-gel hands rolled back the stone;
3. Now no more the cru-el thorn; Glo-ry shall His brow a-dorn;

Songs of glad-ness here we sing To the Lord, our ris-en King.
Je-sus from the grave a-rose, Con-q'ror o'er His might-y foes.
Ev-er-more the ran-somed sing, Vic-t'ry thro' a ris-en King.

Chorus.

Hail! O hail the might-y Conquer-or! Je-sus lives, no more to die,
Oh! shout and sing! O sing the glo-rious vic-to-ry, Let it ech-o thro' the sky.

No. 61. Throw Open the Gates of the City.

J. H. K.   J. H. Kurzenknabe.

1. Throw o-pen the gates of the Cit-y, The beau-ti-ful Cit-y of gold, That the right-cous and ho-ly may en-ter, Where the glo-ries e-ter-nal un-fold.
2. Throw o-pen the gates of the Cit-y, That its light may shine out on the way; For the prod-i-gal, wea-ry of wan-d'ring, Will re-turn to the Fa-ther to-day.
3. Throw o-pen the gates of the Cit-y, To the na-tions in dark-ness and gloom; They are hear-ing the news of sal-va-tion, And glad-ly to Je-sus they come.
4. Throw o-pen the gates of the Cit-y, Let the guests who are bid-den, come in; Soon the Bride-groom and Bride will be read-y, And the feast of the mar-riage be-gin.

Refrain.

Let the light of the won-der-ful Cit-y Guide the pen-i-tents, wea-ry and lone, Till they share the bright glo-ry sur-round-ing The King on His beau-ti-ful throne.

Copyright, 1889, by J. H. Kurzenknabe. Used by per.

The Heavenly Land. Concluded.

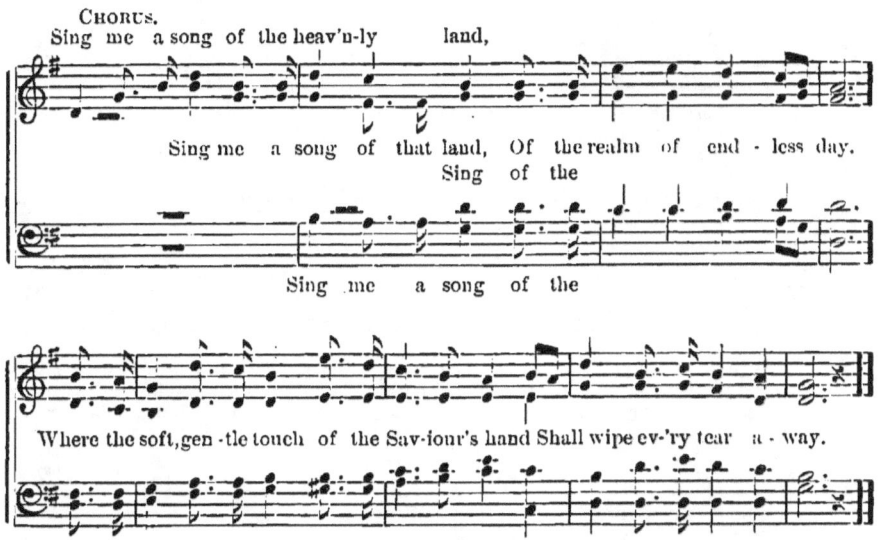

No. 64. Jesus, Tender Shepherd, Hear Me.
A Child's Prayer.

Mrs. Mary Lundie Duncan. Chas. Edw. Prior.

No. 71. **Sabbath Morn has Come.**

ANON. CHAS. EDW. PRIOR.

Speak of it Now. Concluded.

find in the Sav-iour true comfort and peace, Will you not speak of it now?

No. 74. Homeward Bound.

PRISCILLA J. OWENS.　　　　　W. J. KIRKPATRICK.

1. Homeward bound, homeward bound, With the restless waves around; Swift we ride o'er the tide, Je - sus is our guide, Steer - ing for the heav'n-ly land, Palms and lil - ies in each hand; Homeward bound, homeward bound, With the waves around.
2. Watch and pray, watch and pray, Pressing on - ward ev - 'ry day; Rocks are steep, wa - ters deep, Je - sus still will keep; Sing - ing, sail - ing o'er the sea, Je - sus will our Pi - lot be; Watch and pray, watch and pray, Keep the narrow way.
3. Hap - py band, hap - py band, Fol - low on at God's com-mand; Go - ing home, go - ing home, Tho' the bil - lows foam, We are Zi - on's lit - tle fleet, Steer - ing for the gold - en street; Happy band, happy band, Keeping Christ's command.

Copyright, 1881, by John J. Hood. Used by per.

No. 75. "In His Name."

Trio for Female Voices.

Dedicated to "The King's Daughters."

FANNY J. CROSBY.   CHAS. EDW. PRIOR.

1. Of a King we are the daughters, And His roy-al name we bear,
2. Of a King we are the daughters, There is none so great as He,
3. Of a King we are the daughters, And His wealth can ne'er be told,

We are hon-ored with His pres-ence, O-ver-shad-owed by His care;
But His work is vast and bound-less, And we may not i-dle be;
For He dwell-eth in a cit-y That is built of pur-est gold;

He ap-points to each a mis-sion From His dwell-ing-place a-bove,
We must help to lift the bur-dens From the faint-ing and the weak,
There His faith-ful ones shall en-ter, And His bless-ed wel-come share,

"In His Name." Concluded.

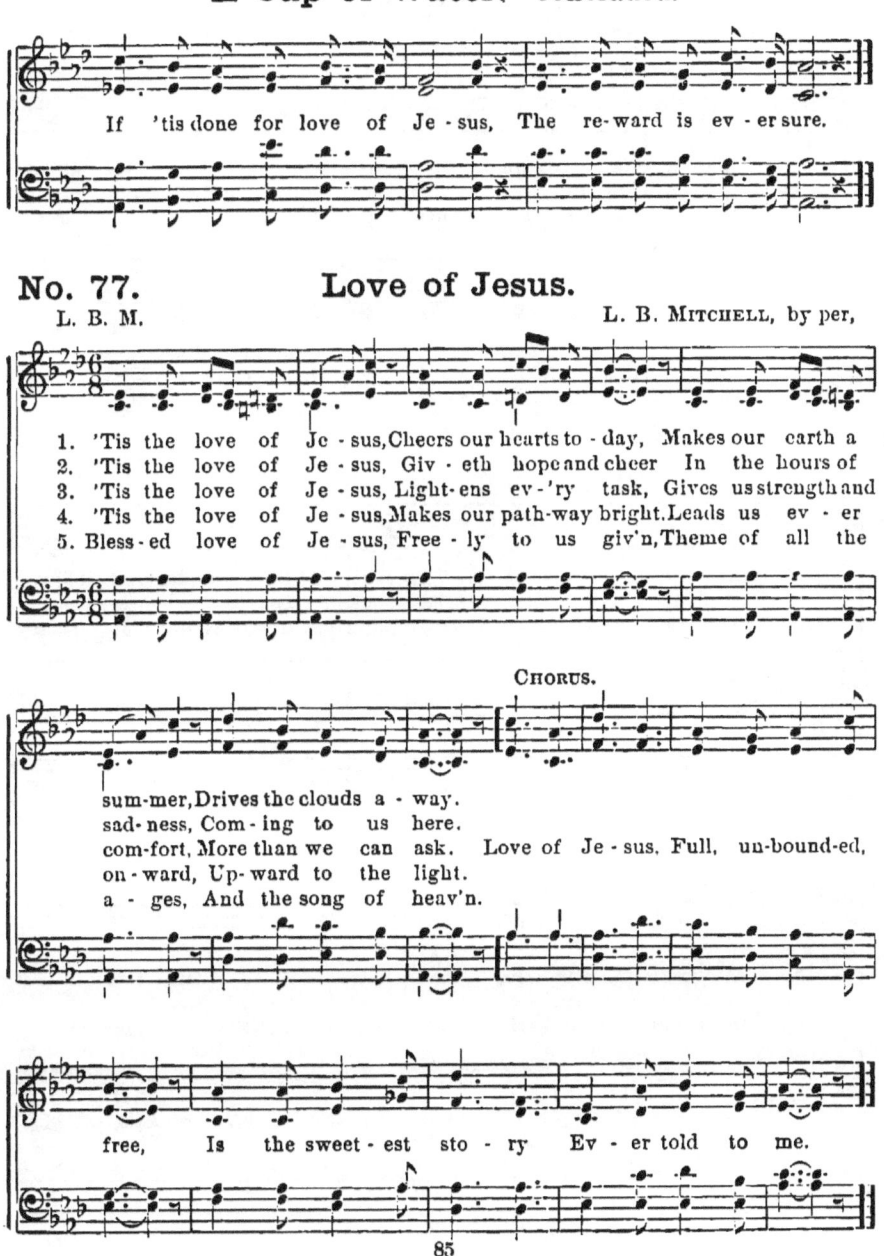

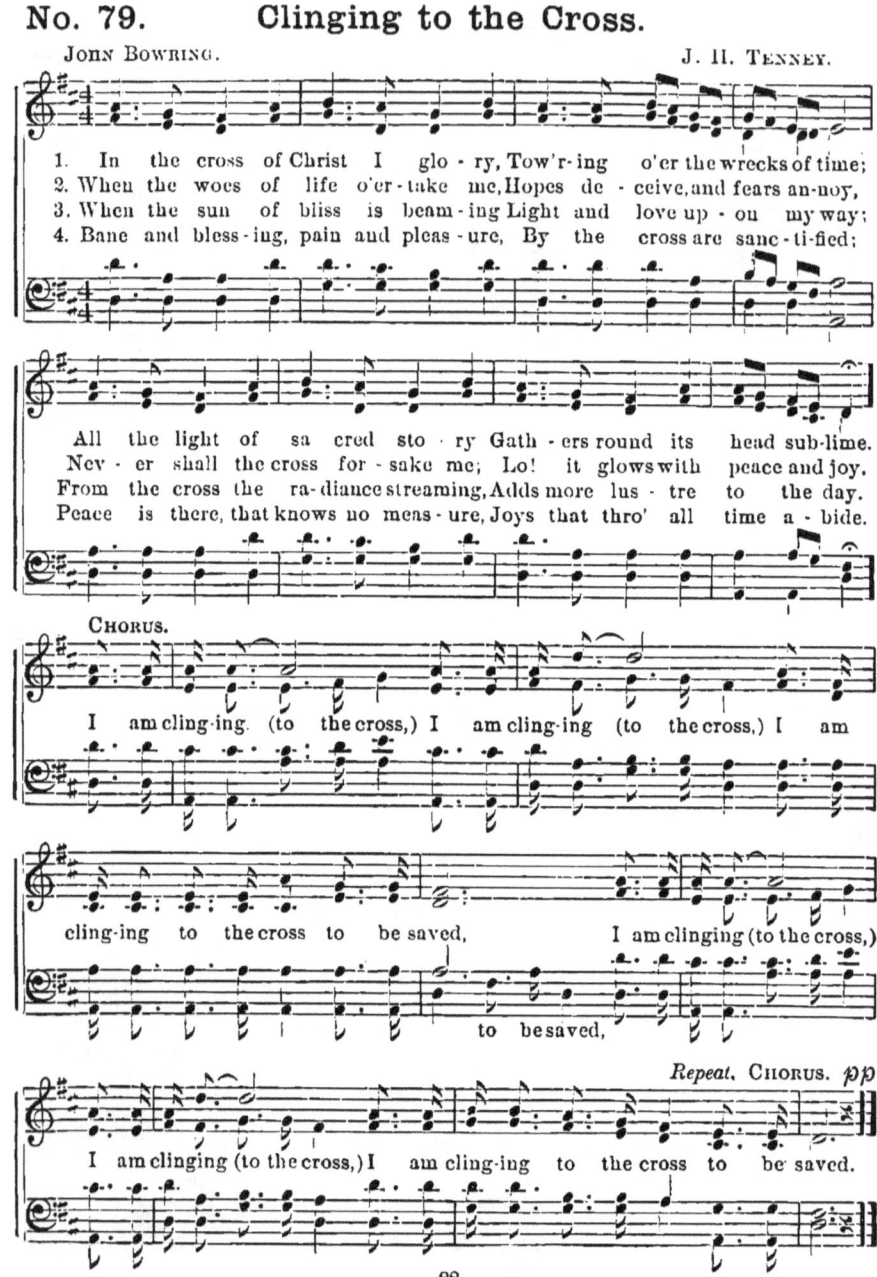

No. 83. The Army of Jesus.

HARRIET E. JONES.   CHAS. EDW. PRIOR.

1. A brave, loy-al ar-my of sol - diers, Is marching with Jesus to-day;
2. Yes, onward this ar-my is march-ing, The "sword of the spirit" in hand;
3. The beau-ti-ful hel-met sal-va - tion, With sandals of peace for their feet,
4. March on, no-ble ar-my of Je - sus, Still shining in gos-pel ar-ray;

Arrayed in the beau-ti - ful ar - mor Of those who the Saviour o-bey.
To "quench" all the "darts of the wicked," That peace may abound in our land.
And faith for their shield, they shall surely The foes of our Saviour de-feat.
Your work shall be felt by the na - tion, And you shall be victors some day.

CHORUS.
This brave Christian ar - my, This glad, conq'ring ar - my, All shin-ing in gos-pel ar - ray, Shall gath-er fresh tro-phies For Je - sus their Cap-tain, While tread-ing the beau - ti - ful way.

Suffer Little Children. Concluded.

such is the kingdom of heav'n, The king-dom of heav'n, the king-dom of heav'n."

No. 86. What can Little Hands Do?

Mrs. Grace W. Hinsdale. Chas. Edw. Prior.

1. O, what can lit-tle *hands* do To please the King of heav'n?
2. O, what can lit-tle *lips* do To please the King of heav'n?
3. O, what can lit-tle *eyes* do To please the King of heav'n?
4. O, what can lit-tle *hearts* do To please the King of heav'n?

The lit-tle hands some work may try, That will some sim-ple
The lit-tle lips can praise and pray, And gen-tle words of
The lit-tle eyes can up-ward look, Can learn to read God's
Young hearts, if He His Spir-it send, Can love Him,—Ma-ker,

want sup-ply; Such grace to mine be giv'n, Such grace to mine be giv'n.
kind-ness say; Such grace to mine be giv'n, Such grace to mine be giv'n.
ho-ly book; Such grace to mine be giv'n, Such grace to mine be giv'n.
Sav-iour, Friend; Such grace to mine be giv'n, Such grace to mine be giv'n.

Copyright, 1883, by J. J. Hood. Used by per.

No. 87. In the Shadow of the Rock.

Rev. Ray Palmer, D.D.   J. H. Tenney.

1. In the shad-ow of the Rock let me rest, (let me rest,) When I feel the tem-pest's shock thrill my breast; (thrill my breast;) All in vain the storm shall sweep while I hide, (while I hide,) And my tran-quil sta-tion keep at Thy side, (at Thy side.)
2. I in peace will rest me there till I see, (till I see,) That the skies a-gain are fair o-ver me, (o-ver me,) That the burn-ing heats are past, and the day, (and the day,) Bids the trav-el-er at last go his way, (go his way.)
3. Then my pil-grim staff I'll take and once more, (and once more,) I'll my on-ward jour-ney make as be-fore, (as be-fore,) And with joy-ous heart and strong I will raise, (I will raise,) Un-to Thee, O Rock, a song glad with praise,(glad with praise.)

CHORUS.

Then let me rest, then let me rest, In the shad-ow of the Rock, In the shad-ow of the Rock let me rest, (let me rest,) Then let me rest,.... In the

Copyright, 1880, by John J. Hood. From "Words of Life," by per.

No. 89. What shall We bring?

Mrs. E. C. Ellsworth. Chas. Edw. Prior.

1. Oh, what shall we bring to the Master, Who deal-eth so kind-ly and true? Our hands are now full of His bless-ings, Be-stowed up-on me and on you,
2. Oh, what shall we bring to the Master, Whose love for us en-tered the grave? Who fought for our foes and subdued them, Who died that our souls He might save,
3. Oh, what shall we bring to the Master, Who sought us while go-ing a-stray? Who guid-eth our wan-der-ing foot-steps, To re-gions where dwelleth the day,

CHORUS.

We'll bring Him our time and our tal-ents, We'll bring Him a heart-ser-vice sweet, We'll bring Him the best and the bright-est, Our all we will lay at His feet.

By per. of E. O. Excell, owner of Copyright, Chicago, Ill.

No. 90. In the Shadow of the Cross.

E. R. Latta. J. H. Tenney.

1. There's a place above all others Where my spirit loves to be;
2. On the cross my Saviour suffered, That He might atone for me;
3. When my heart is full of trouble, Then I love, on bended knee,
4. Blessed Saviour, Thou wilt hear me When I make my earnest plea,

'Tis within the sacred shadow Of the cross of Calvary.
And I love the blessed shadow Of the cross of Calvary.
To approach him, in the shadow Of the cross of Calvary.
If I kneel within the shadow Of the cross of Calvary.

CHORUS.

In the shadow of the cross, In the shadow of the cross, There my spirit loves to be, In the shadow of the cross.

Copyright, 1883, by J. H. Tenney.

Come unto Me. Concluded.

"Come and lean up-on my breast, Come...... un-to me."......
"I will give you peace and rest, Come un-to me, come un-to me."

No. 92. I Shall Be Whiter than Snow.

Rev. E. A. Hoffman. J. H. Tenney.

1. Thy grace, O my Sav-iour, can reach ev-en me! I know that, if
2. My soul is all weak-ness, my heart is un-clean, But Thy precious
3. I'll doubt Thee no long-er, this mo-ment I'll go, And wash in the

Chorus.

washed in Thy blood I shall be Whit-er than snow, yes, whit-er than
blood can re-deem from all sin.
blood that makes whit-er than snow.

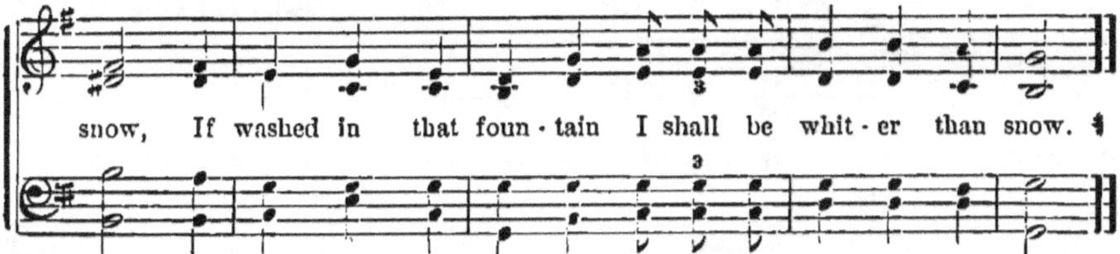

snow, If washed in that foun-tain I shall be whit-er than snow.

Copyright, 1878, by J. H. Tenney.

No. 94. Where He Leads I'll Follow.

"Come unto Me, all ye that labor and are heavy laden, and I will give you rest." Matt. 11:28.

W. A. O.   W. A. Ogden.

1. Sweet are the prom-is-es, Kind is the word; Dear-er far than an-y mes-sage man ev-er heard, Pure was the mind of Christ, Sin-less I see; He the great ex-am-ple is, and pat-tern for me.

2. Sweet is the ten-der love Je-sus hath shown; Sweet-er far than an-y love that mor-tals have known, Kind to the err-ing one, Faith-ful is he; He the great ex-am-ple is, and pat-tern for me.

3. List to His lov-ing words, "Come un-to me." Wea-ry, heavy lad-en, there is sweet rest for thee, Trust in His prom-is-es, Faith-ful and sure; Lean up-on the Sav-iour, and thy soul is se-cure.

CHORUS.

Where............ He leads I'll fol - - low,
Where He leads I'll fol-low,   Where He leads I'll fol low,

Fol - - low all the way,   Fol low Je-sus ev-'ry day.
Fol-low all the way, yes, fol-low all the way.

Copyright, 1885, by W. A. Ogden. Used by per.

All Things are Yours. Concluded.

REFRAIN.

All things are yours! All things are yours! Let songs of rap-ture ring! of rapture ring!

O heir with Christ, all things are yours! O hap-py child of a King!

No. 96. Nearing the Better Land.

W. A. SPATE. J. H. TENNEY.

1. Care-worn trav'ler on life's o-cean, Bound for yon-der gold-en strand,
2. Tho' the sky be dark and gloom-y, And the wild storms loudly roar,
3. Trust in God and be not fear-ful, He will lend a help-ing hand,

Look beyond the wave's com-mo-tion, Thou art near-ing that blest land.
Look with hopeful heart be-yond them, Thou art near-ing yon blest land.
Let thy heart be light and cheer-ful; Thou art near the bet-ter land.

REFRAIN.

Near-ing, near-ing, near-ing, near-ing, Thou art near-ing that blest land.

From "Songs of Joy," by per.

No. 97. O Come, Let Us Worship.

IDA L. REED. CHAS. EDW. PRIOR.

1. O come let us wor-ship our Sav-iour and King, The Sav-iour so gen-tle, yet might-y to save, We'll kneel at His feet and His prais-es we'll sing Who for us hath tri-umphed o'er death and the grave.
2. To-day let us come ere the night-shad-ows fall, And bring to the Sav-iour our tri-bute of love, To Je-sus, our Shep-herd, our soul's "all in all," Who reigneth in peace o'er the king-dom a-bove.
3. With songs of re-joic-ing and hearts full of cheer, We come in life's morn-ing to our bless-ed friend; With His ban-ner o'er us, we'll know not a fear, His arm fail-eth nev-er, He loves to the end.

REFRAIN.

O! praise Him for-ev-er, blest Sav-iour and King, Who pur-chased our souls with His own pre-cious blood; All o-ver the earth let His

*Small notes and octaves for instrument. Bass will sing upper notes of octaves.

O Come, Let Us Worship. Concluded.

glad prais-es ring, Till all may be washed in the sin-cleans-ing flood.

No. 98. Jesus, I Come to Thee.

E. A. Hoffman.   D. F. Hodges.

1. Je-sus, I come to Thee, Thou hast in-vit-ed me; Hum-bly and
2. Je-sus, I come to Thee, Knowing Thou lov-est me, For Thou hast
3. Je-sus, I come to Thee, Long-ing for pu-ri-ty; Now, Sav-iour,
4. Je-sus, I come to Thee, Thy blood my on-ly plea; See how im-

trust-ing-ly   I come to Thee,
pur-chased me   On Cal-va-ry,
cleanse Thou me,   I come to Thee,
plor-ing-ly   I come to Thee,

CHORUS.

Help me to come, Je-sus, Help me to come, Reach me Thy hand, Je-sus, Help me to come,

Golden Gates, Concluded.

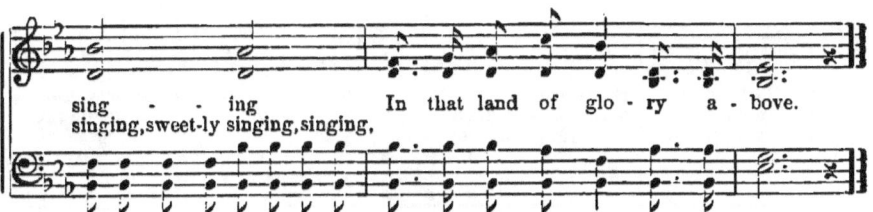

sing - - ing In that land of glo-ry a-bove.
singing, sweet-ly singing, singing,

No. 100. Praises to our Saviour King.

"I will sing praises unto the Lord." Ps. 27: 6.

C. W. R. CHAS. EDW. PRIOR.

1. Sav-iour King, I would sing To Thy praise and glo-ry,
2. Once to die, from on high Thou did'st come to woo me;
3. From the dead Thou hast led Death in chains for-ev-er:

O'er and o'er, ev-er-more, Sing re-demp-tion's sto-ry;
While I live I would give Life and be-ing to Thee;
Now a-bove, from Thy love Naught my soul can sev-er;

Thou did'st bear the cross for me; I would give my-self to Thee.
Teach me all Thy ho-ly will, All Thy pleas-ure to ful-fill.
Let all earth and heav-en sing Prais-es to our Sav-iour King.

Copyright, 1883, by John J. Hood. By per.

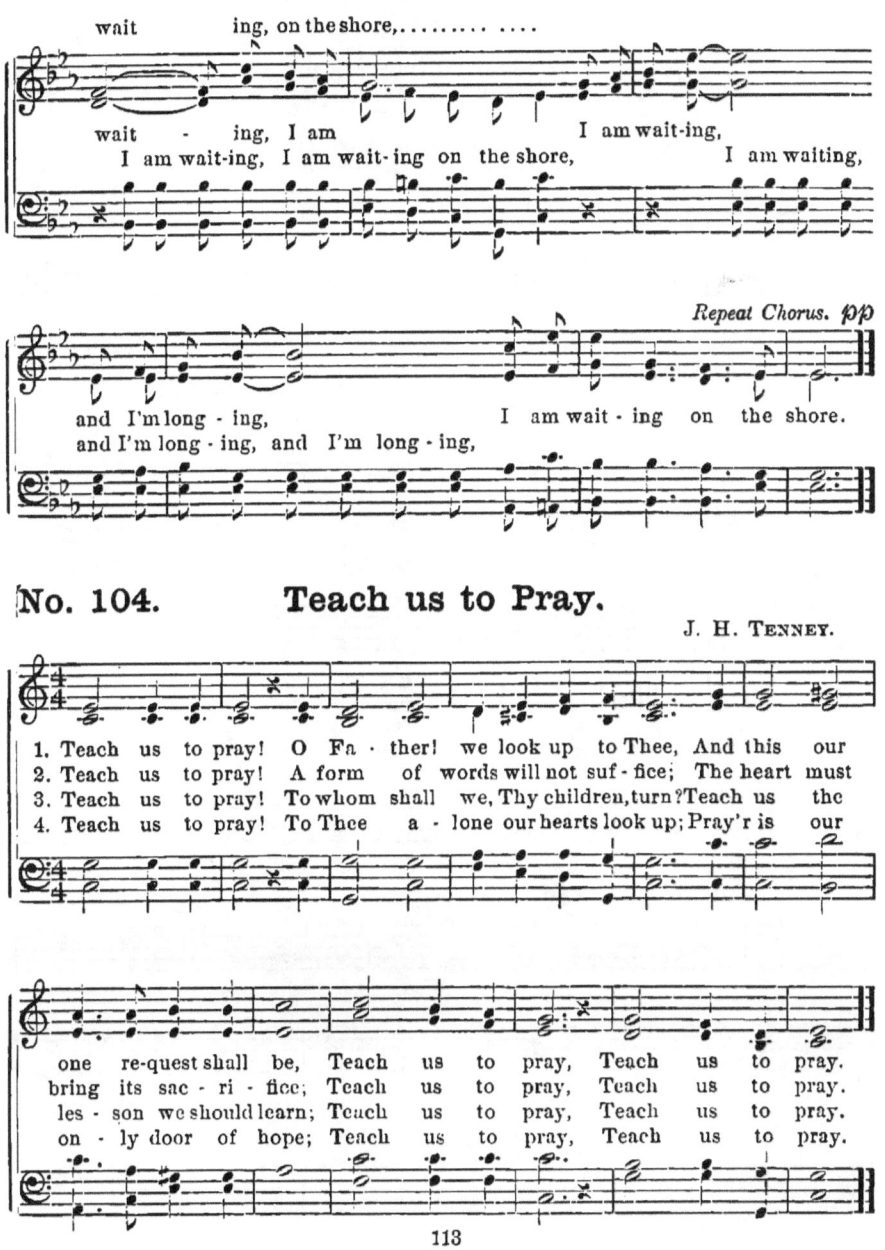

No. 105. I will follow Jesus.

Infant Class

J. H. Tenney, by per.

1. The world is ver-y beau-ti-ful, And full of joy to me;
2. I'm but a lit-tle pil-grim, My jour-ney's just be-gun:
3. Then, like a lit-tle pil-grim, What-ev-er I may meet,
4. Then tri-als can-not vex me, And pain I need not fear;

The sun shines out in glo-ry, On ev-'ry-thing I see;
They say I shall meet sor-row Be-fore my jour-ney's done,
I'll take it,— joy or sor-row,—And lay at Je-sus' feet;
For when I'm close by Je-sus, Grief can-not come too near,

I know I shall be hap-py While in the world I stay,
The world is full of sor-row And suf-fer-ing, they say,
He'll com-fort me in trou-ble, He'll wipe my tears a-way,
Not e-ven death can harm me; When death I meet one day,

For I will fol-low Je-sus, Will fol-low all the way,
But I will fol-low Je-sus, Will fol-low all the way,
With joy I'll fol-low Je-sus, Will fol-low all the way,
To heav'n I'll fol-low Je-sus, Will fol-low all the way,

Chorus.

For I will fol-low Je-sus, For I will fol-low Je-sus,

For I will fol-low Je-sus, Will fol-low all the way,

No. 106. **The Hours of Day are over.**
Evening Hymn.

H. P. DANKS. By per.

1. The hours of day are o-ver, The eve-ning calls us home;
   Once more to Thee, O Fa-ther, with thank-ful hearts we come;
   For all Thy count-less bless-ings We praise Thy ho-ly Name,
   And own Thy love un chang-ing, Thro' days and years the same.

2. For life, and health, and shel-ter, From harm thro' out the day,
   The kind-ness of our teach-ers in point-ing out the way;
   For all the dear af-fec-tion Of pa-rents, broth-ers, friends,
   To Him our thanks we ren-der, Who these, and all things sends.

3. But these, O Lord, can show us Thy good-ness but in part;
   Thy love would lead us on-ward to know Thee as thou art;
   Thy Son came down from heav-en To take a-way our sin,
   Thy Spir-it dwells a-mong us To make us clean with-in.

4 For this, O Lord, we bless Thee,
  For this we thank Thee most:—
  The cleansing of the sinful,
  The saving of the lost;
  The Teacher ever present,
  The Friend forever nigh,
  The home prepared by Jesus
  For us above the sky.

5 Lord, gather all Thy children
  To meet Thee there at last,
  When earthly tasks are ended,
  And earthly days are past;
  With all our dear ones round us
  In that eternal home,
  Where death no more shall part us,
  And night shall never come.

No. 108. I will Give you Rest.

IDA L. REED. CHAS. EDW. PRIOR.

Jesus Shall Reign. Concluded.

Je - sus shall reign when time shall be no more.
Glo - ry to God, e - ter - nal, Three in One.

No. 110. Precious Blood of Jesus.

FRANCES RIDLEY HAVERGAL.   J. H. TENNEY.

1. Pre - cious, pre - cious blood of Je - sus, Shed on Cal - va - ry,
2. Pre - cious, pre - cious blood of Je - sus, Let it make thee whole;
3. Tho' thy sins are red like crim - son, Deep in scar - let glow,
4. Now the ho - li - est with bold - ness We may en - ter in,

Fine.

Shed for reb - els, shed for sin - ners, Shed for me.
Let it flow in might - y cleans - ing O'er my soul.
Je - sus' pre - cious blood will wash thee White as snow.
For the o - pened foun - tain cleans - eth From all sin.

D.S. Oh, be - lieve it, oh, re - ceive it, 'Tis for thee!

CHORUS.   *D. S.*

Pre - cious, pre - cious blood of Je - sus, Ev - er flowing free!

Used by per. of Oliver Ditson Co., owner of copyright.

No. 111. Why not Trust in Him Now?

Mrs. E. W. Chapman. J. H. Tenney, by per.

1. The Sav-iour hath called thee and shown thee His love; He died for poor sin-ners like thee; He left His bright home in the man-sions a-bove, The cap-tive from bon-dage to free.
2. His blood He hath shed to re-deem thee from sin; A fount has been o-pened for thee; He tells thee of heav-en and bids thee come in, The beau-ties of E-den to see.
3. He'll clothe thee with ves-ture that's whit-er than snow; In pas-tures of ver-dure will lead, Where wa-ters of life in a-bun-dance do flow, Thy soul in its rap-tures to feed.

CHORUS.

Oh, why not trust in Him now?.......... Oh, why not trust in Him now?..........
trust in Him now? trust in Him now?
He loves thee and bids thee on Him to re-ly; Oh, why not trust in Him now?....
trust in Him now?

No. 112. Who Will Win?

Rev. C. W. Ray. D. D.   Chas. Edw. Prior.

With martial spirit and enthusiasm.

1. 'Tis not for pleas-ure du-ty calls To ral-ly forth in arms,
2. 'Tis not the pomp of dress par-ade, With mar-tial prow-ess rife;
3. Tho' fierce the on-set of the foe, With cour-age we must stand;
4. Let us be ev-er brave and true, In bat-tle for the right;

Nor shout, nor song the foe ap-palls, Nor march with trum-pet charms.
Nor nois-y tramp of cav-al-cade, That ends the fear-ful strife.
We soon shall see his o-ver-throw, If strong of heart and hand.
And by the faith-ful work we do, Keep all our ar-mor bright.

Chorus.

Who-e'er would win the vic-to-ry, Must watch, and work and pray, 'Tis
must watch and work and pray,
toil that brings the ju-bi-lee, That gains for us the day.

No. 114. Life, Eternal Life.

PRISCILLA J. OWENS. FRANK M. DAVIS.

1. O, tell me not to pause, vain world, O bid me not de-lay;
2. Your gold as dross, your gain as loss, In heav-en's light dis-cern;
3. I hear the voice of Je-sus call, His guid-ing light I see;

I seek a bet-ter home be-yond, And up-ward is my way.
I glad-ly take my Saviour's cross, And all your pleas-ures spurn.
O do not call me back, my friends, But come and walk with me.

CHORUS.

Life! Life! e-ter-nal Life! The glo-rious prize I see;

Life! Life! e-ter-nal Life! That is the prize for me....

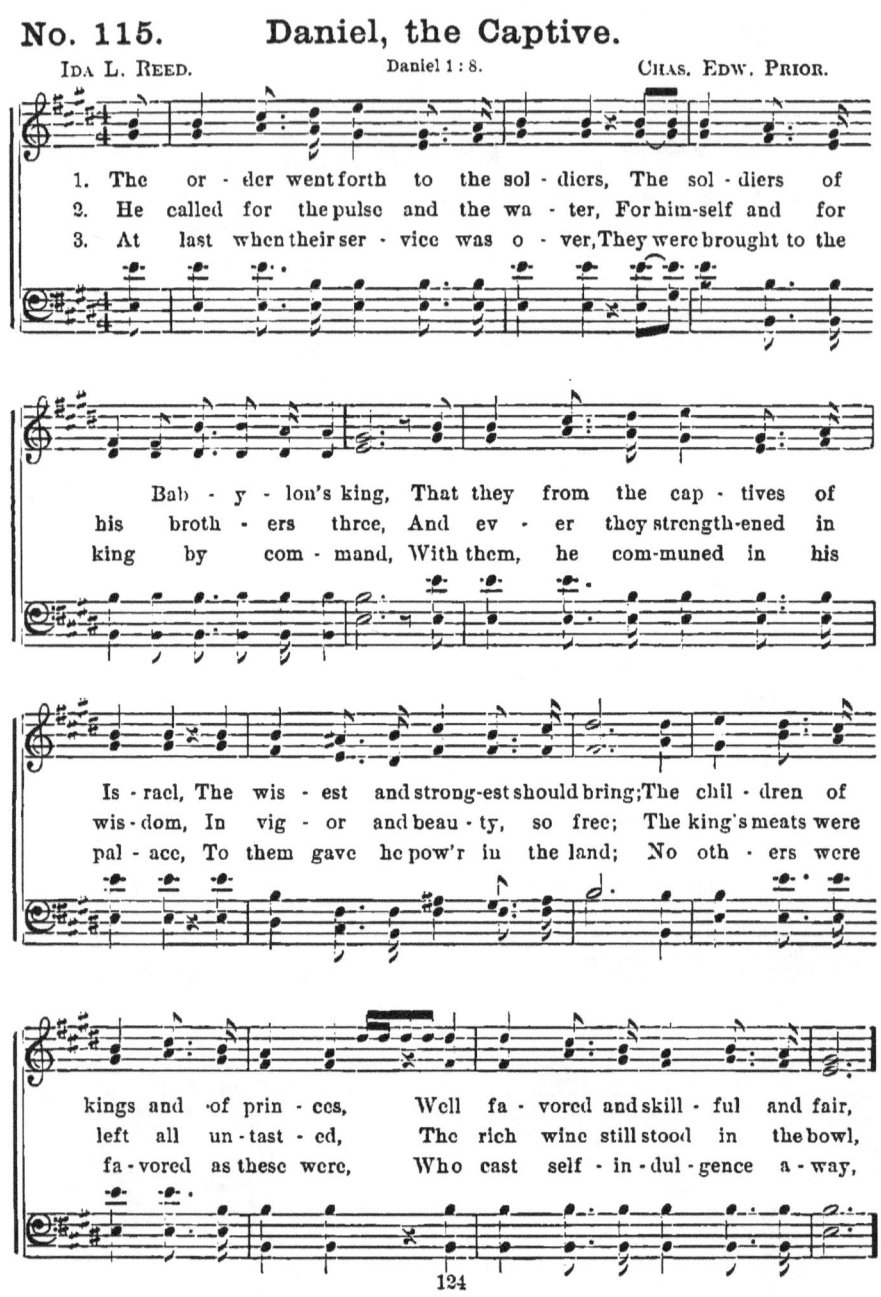

Daniel, the Captive. Concluded.

To stud-y the Chal-de-an's teach-ings, And stand in his pal-ace there.
For he would not pam-per his bod-y, Nor hin-der the growth of his soul,
God save them all knowledge and wisdom, And strengthened their spirits each day,

CHORUS.

It was Dan-iel, a cap-tive a-mong them, Who in his heart pur-posed to spare Him-self and his brethren, from be-ing De-filed by the king's cho-sen fare.

No. 116. A Voice from Heaven.

W. A. OGDEN.

1. Hark! a voice from heav-en From the Ho-ly One, "This is my be-lov-ed, Well be-lov-ed Son," Hear Him and be-lieve Him, That He speaks is true,'Tis a mes-sage from the Fa-ther un-to you.
2. Lo! a bless-ed Spir-it! Lo, the Heav'nly Dove! On our Lord de-scend-ing From the heav'ns a-bove, "This is my be-lov-ed," Hear the voice proclaim, "This is my be-lov-ed Son, oh! hear ye Him."
3. Let the earth re-ceive Him, Let the na-tions sing, Glo-ry, hal-le-lu-jah, "Je-sus is our King!" O-ver death tri-um-phant, O-ver all His foes, From the grave vic-to-ri-ous He rose! He rose!

D. S. Fol-low Him right glad-ly, In the days of youth, He is thy ex-am-ple, Full of grace and truth.

CHORUS.

"This is my be-lov-ed, my well be-lov-ed Son," Je-sus Christ, the right-eous, Him, the liv-ing One!

By per. of the Author.

Ho! Every one that Thirsteth. Concluded.

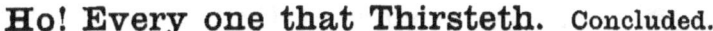

O come, and take of it free-ly, Beau-ti-ful wa-ter of life.

No. 119. Jesus is Precious.

"A friend that sticketh closer than a brother." Prov. 18 ; 24.

F. M. D.   Frank M. Davis.

1. Jesus is precious, precious to me, Thro' His dear name my soul was made free; He is my ref-uge, safe-ty, re-treat, Rest-ing in Him is glo-ry com-plete.
2. Jesus is precious, precious to me, This is my song and ev-er shall be; No oth-er friend to me is so dear, His is a love that cast-eth out fear.
3. Jesus is precious, precious to me, I will pro-claim it o'er land and sea; Gen-tly His Spir-it leads me a-long, Fill-ing my soul with this joy-ous song.

D. S. I will ex-alt His name ev-er-more, Whom ser-aphs praise and an-gels a-dore.

Fine. Chorus.

Jesus is precious, precious to me; Glory to God! His blood set me free.

D. S.

No. 120. On the Cross at Calvary.

W. S. M.   W. S. Martin, by per.

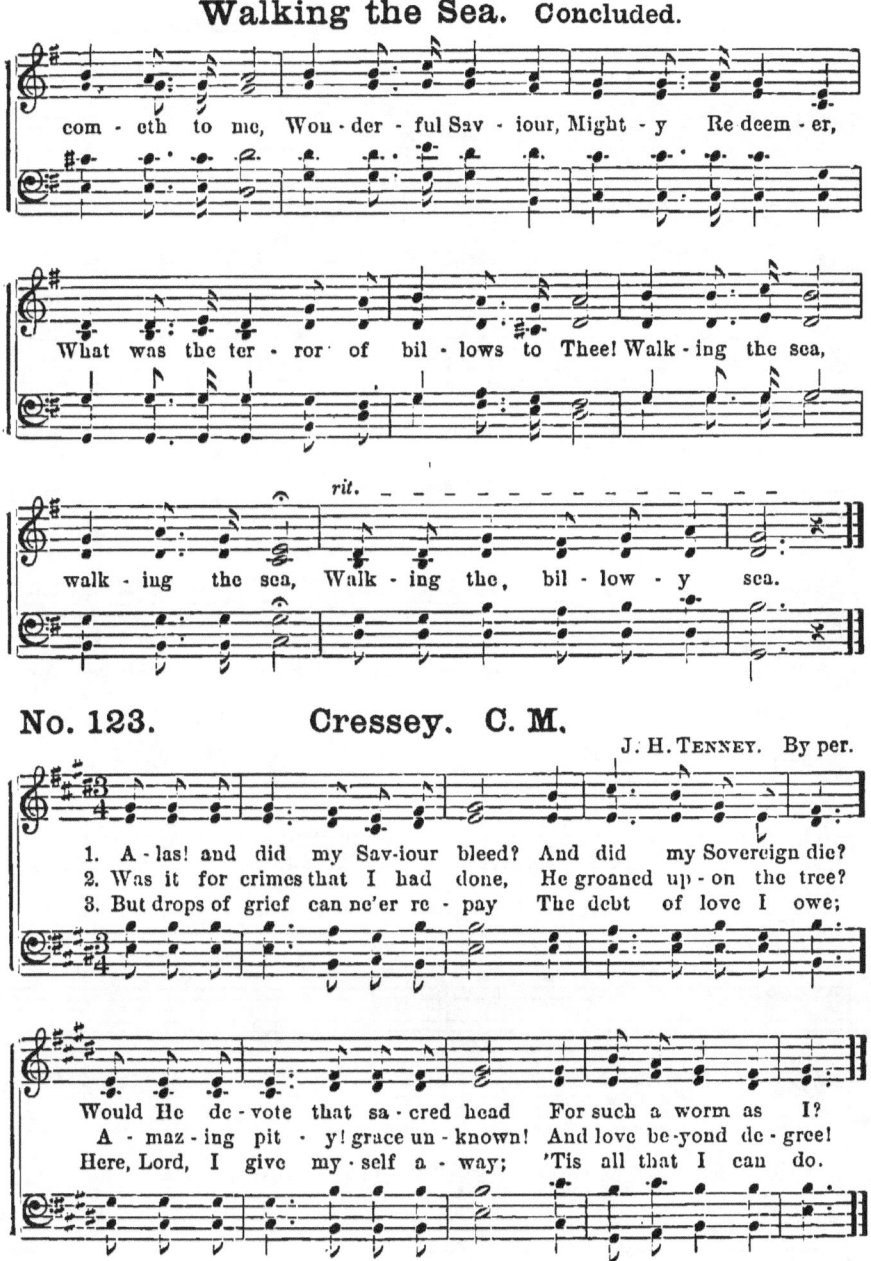

Where they Never say Farewell. Concluded.

'Twill be sweet, oh, sweet to dwell Where they nev-er say fare-well!

No. 125. Ever will I pray.

"Evening, morning, and at noon will I pray." Psa. 55: 17.

A. CUMMINGS.   J. H. TENNEY.

1. Fa-ther, in the morn-ing Un-to Thee I'll pray; Let Thy lov-ing
2. At the bus-y noon-tide, Press'd with work and care, Then I'll wait with
3. When the eve-ning shad-ows Chase a-way the light, Fa-ther, then I'll
4. Thus in life's glad morn-ing, In its bright noon-day, In its shadowy

CHORUS.

kind-ness, Keep me thro' this day. I will pray, I will pray, Ev-er
Je-sus Till He hear my pray'r.
pray Thee, Bless Thy child to-night.
eve-ning, Ev-er will I pray. I will pray, I will pray,

will I pray; Morn-ing, noon and eve-ning, Un-to Thee I'll pray,
Ev-er will I pray;

Copyright, 1879, by J. H. Tenney.

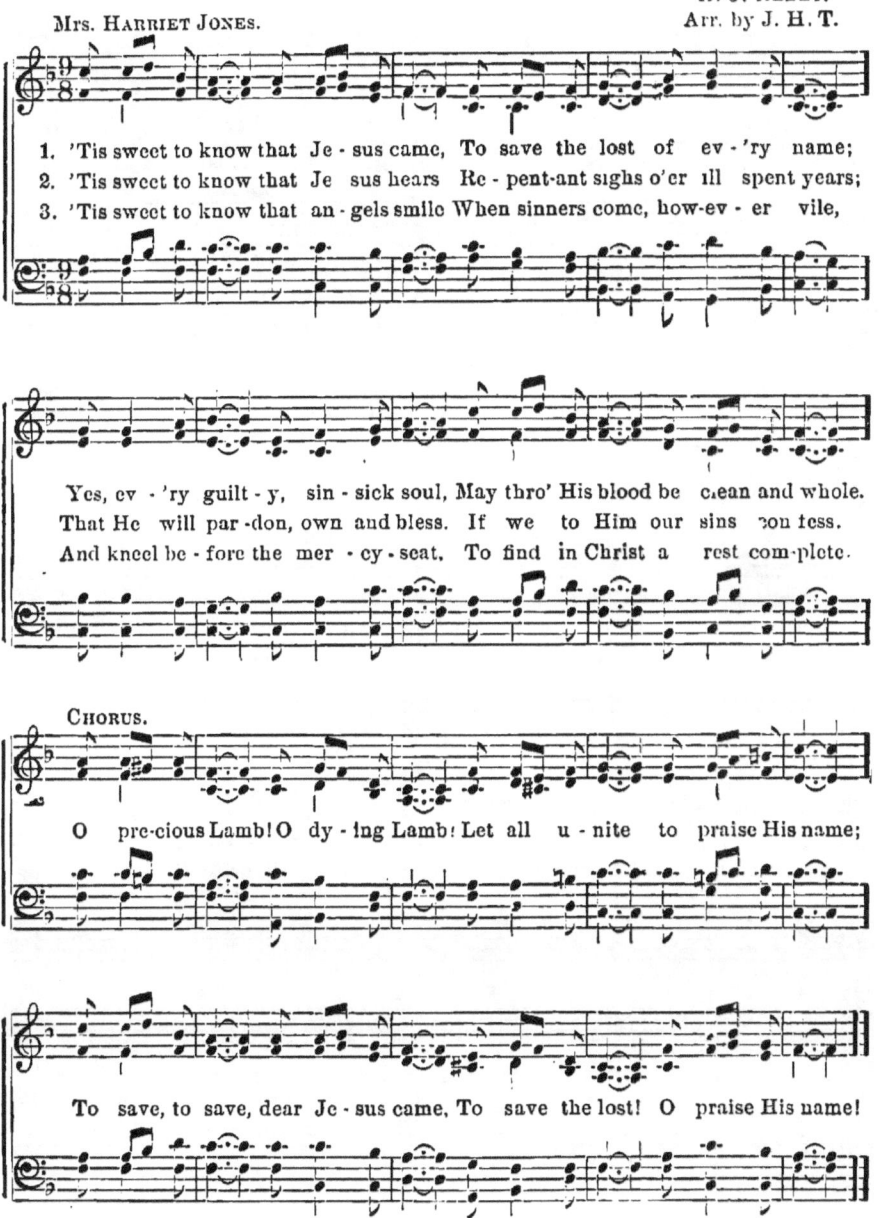

No. 129. My Own Dear Father-land.

W. S. Martin.   J. H. Tenney, by per.

1. There is a bright home just be-yond the wea-ry years, With free-dom from sor-row and care, Where Je-sus, the Sav-iour, shall wipe a-way our tears, And with Him His glo-ry to share.
2. No dark-ness have they who have reached that world a-bove; No need of the sun or the moon; They bask in the pres-ence of God's e-ter-nal love, And mid-night to them is as noon.
3. O has-ten to share in the joy that knows no end, With Je-sus, my Sav-iour, at home; This pray'r from my heart un-to Him shall now as-cend, De-lay not, my Mas-ter, but come.

CHORUS.

This happy place is my own dear Father-land; By faith 'mid its pleasures I roam, With dear ones of earth, who have joined the happy band, To rest in that heav'nly home.

No. 131. Shining for Jesus.
For the little ones.

IDA L. REED.   C. K. LANGLEY.

1. We're shin-ing for Je-sus, our Sav-iour, Tho' lit-tle and weak we may be,
2. We're shin-ing for Je-sus, our Sav-iour, We're number'd a-mong the glad throng
3. We're shin-ing for Je-sus, our Sav-iour, Tho' small are the deeds we can do,

Yet some-way we dai-ly can serve Him, Whose love for us flow-eth so free.
Of chil-dren who own Him their ref-uge, And praise Him thro' work, pray'r and song.
By such we can learn to be faith-ful, And keep our lights stead-y and true.

CHORUS.   our Sav-iour,   a - bove......

We're shining for Jesus, for Je-sus our Saviour, Who reigneth all princes, all princes above,

                                                                                              a - bove......

And dai-ly grow stronger and bet-ter,.... By serv-ing the Master we love.
                  yes, stronger and better,

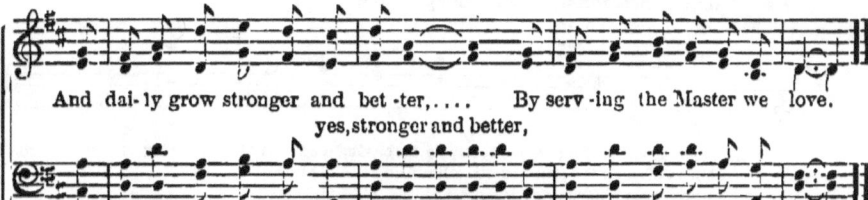

Why the Saviour Loves Me So. Concluded.

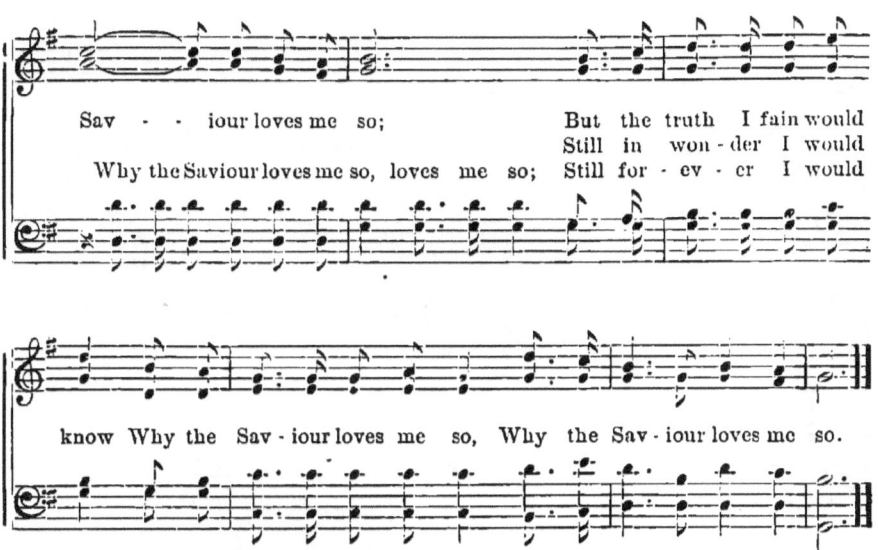

No. 135.   The Lord's Prayer.

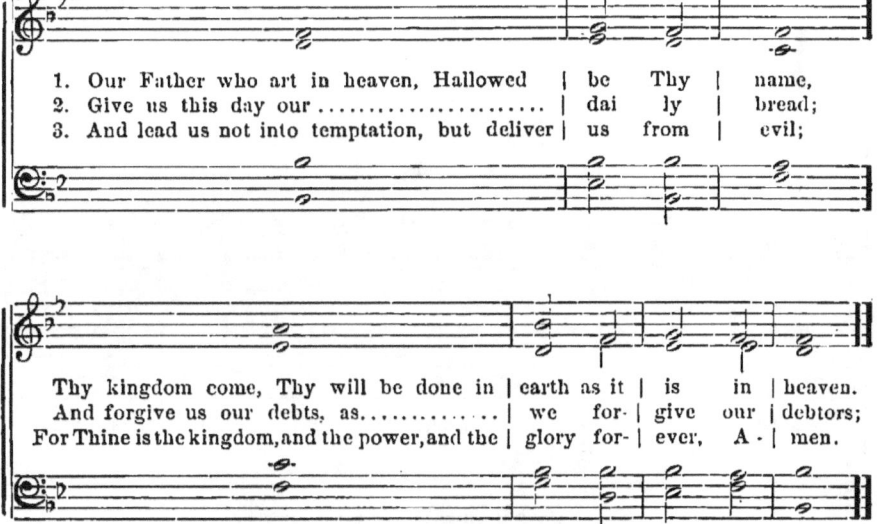

1. Our Father who art in heaven, Hallowed | be | Thy | name,
2. Give us this day our .... | dai- | ly | bread;
3. And lead us not into temptation, but deliver | us | from | evil;

Thy kingdom come, Thy will be done in | earth as it | is | in | heaven.
And forgive us our debts, as.............. | we for- | give | our | debtors;
For Thine is the kingdom, and the power, and the | glory for- | ever, | A- | men.

No. 138. Star and Song.

Trio and Chorus, for Christmas.

E. A. Barnes. Chas. Edw. Prior.

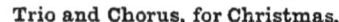

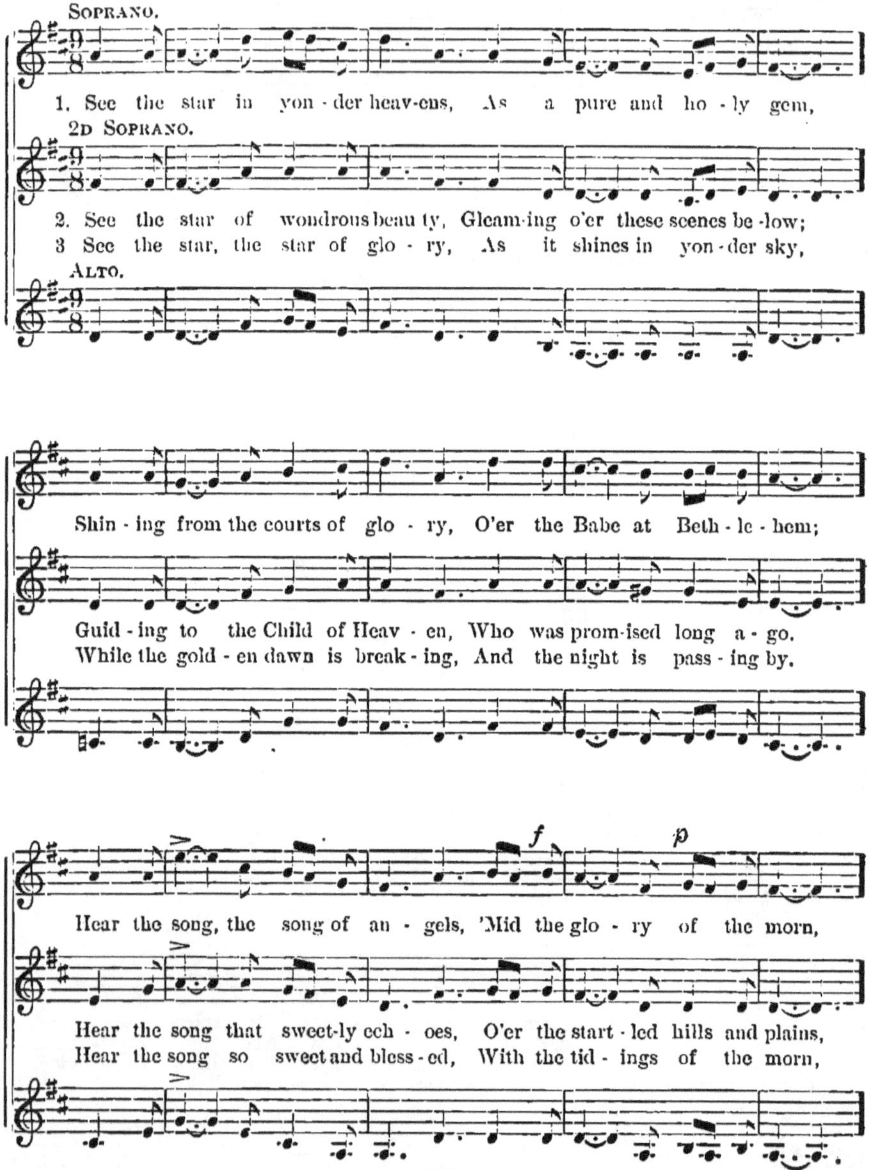
Soprano.
1. See the star in yon - der heav-ens, As a pure and ho - ly gem,
2d Soprano.
2. See the star of wondrous beau ty, Gleam-ing o'er these scenes be -low;
3 See the star, the star of glo - ry, As it shines in yon - der sky,
Alto.
Shin - ing from the courts of glo - ry, O'er the Babe at Beth - le - hem;
Guid - ing to the Child of Heav - en, Who was prom-ised long a - go.
While the gold - en dawn is break - ing, And the night is pass - ing by.
Hear the song, the song of an - gels, 'Mid the glo - ry of the morn,
f
p
Hear the song that sweet-ly ech - oes, O'er the start - led hills and plains,
Hear the song so sweet and bless - ed, With the tid - ings of the morn,

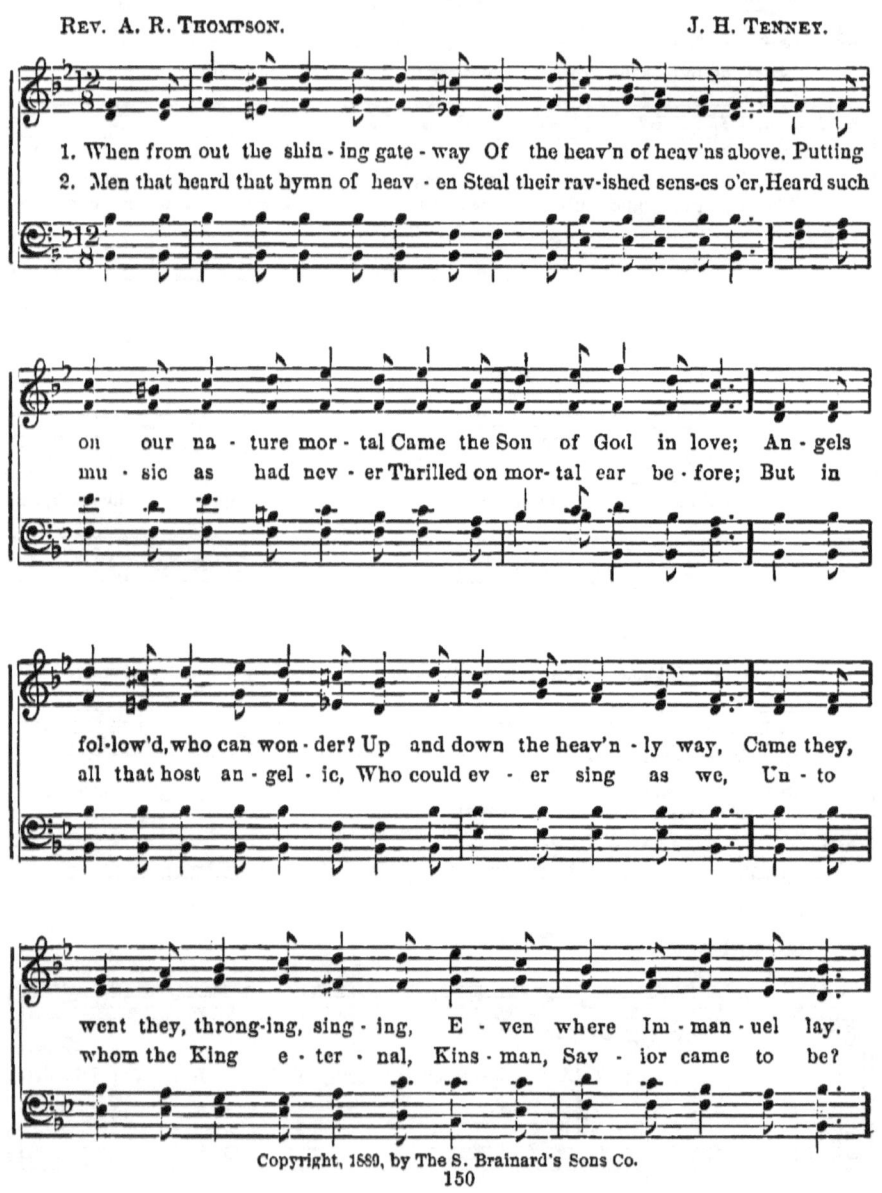

At the Blest Nativity. Concluded.

No. 140. Oh! Hear the Angels' Song.

For Christmas.

T. P. W.
Thos. P. Westendorf.

1. Hear how the an-gels sing Glad the mes-sage now they bring; Sweet peace to earth is sent, Sweet-est peace and blest con-tent, Christ who was born to-day, Takes our ev-'ry sin a-way.
2. Far in the east-ern skies See the star of glo-ry rise; Bright star of Beth-le-hem, Shin-ing like a di-a-dem, While from the an-gel band Comes a might-y cho-rus grand:
3. See now the wise men led To the Sav-ior's man-ger bed, And at His in-fant feet Bow in ad-o-ra-tion sweet; Still from the an-gel choir Comes these words like burn-ing fire:

"Glo-ry in the high-est, glo-ry, Peace, good-will to men."

CHORUS.

Oh, hear.......... the an-gels song! They sing.......... it
Hear the angel's song, Hear the angel's song! Sing it now a-gain,

Copyright, 1889, by The S. Brainard's Sons Co.

Oh! Hear the Angels' Song. Concluded.

No. 141. Ring out each Chiming Bell.

PRISCILLA J. OWENS.   Christmas Song.   CHAS. EDW. PRIOR.

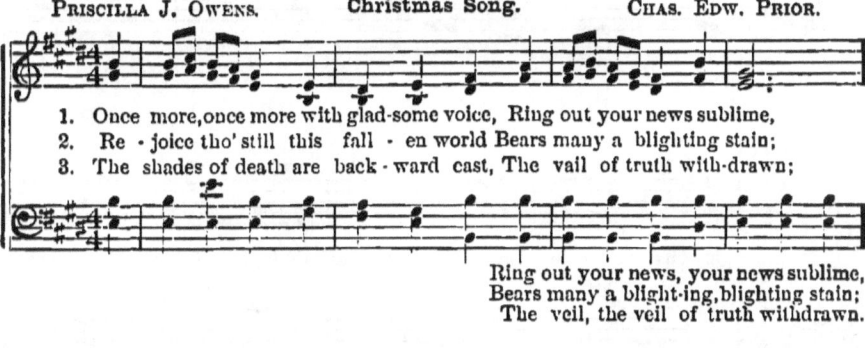

1. Once more, once more with glad-some voice, Ring out your news sublime,
2. Re-joice tho' still this fall-en world Bears many a blighting stain;
3. The shades of death are back-ward cast, The vail of truth with-drawn;

Ring out your news, your news sublime,
Bears many a blight-ing, blighting stain;
The veil, the veil of truth withdrawn.

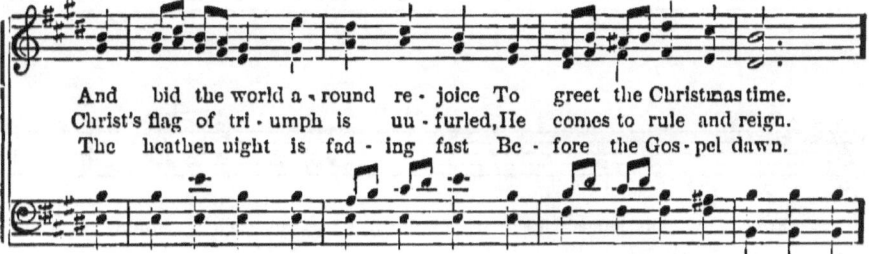

And bid the world a-round re-joice To greet the Christmas time.
Christ's flag of tri-umph is un-furled, He comes to rule and reign.
The heathen night is fad-ing fast Be-fore the Gos-pel dawn.

To greet, to greet the Christmas time.
He comes, He comes to rule and reign.
Be-fore, be-fore the Gos-pel dawn.

Copyright, 1889, by The S. Brainard's Sons Co.

No. 143. All Hail, Mighty Saviour!

Priscilla J. Owens.   Easter.   Chas. Edw. Prior.

1. The Sav-iour was sleep-ing, His followers were weep-ing, Their hopes had gone down in the gloom of the grave; But glo-ry was dawn-ing to bright-en the morning, To light His up-ris-ing, Al-mighty to save.
2. Oh! ye who are griev-ing, come near-er be-liev-ing, The grave could not hold Him who made earth and skies! An an-gel from glo-ry, pro-claims the glad sto-ry, "He go-eth be-fore you," Then lift up your eyes.
3. He go-eth be-fore us, His ban-ner is o'er us, Lead on, bless-ed Mas-ter till glo-ry shall dawn! Since Thou hast as-cend-ed, our fears are all end-ed, Our hopes are tri-um-phant This glad Eas-ter morn.

CHORUS.

All hail, mighty Sav-iour, ex-alt-ed for-ev-er, Who en-tered death's kingdom its chains to de-stroy; Now Christ has a-ris-en, Now

All Hail, Mighty Saviour! Concluded.

Christ has a-ris-en, Ye souls that seek Je-sus shall find Him with joy.

No. 144.   **Goodwin. 7 & 6s.**

G. J. WEBB.

1. Stand up, stand up for Je - sus, Ye sol - diers of the cross; Lift
high His roy - al ban - ner, It must not suf - fer loss;
ev - 'ry foe is van-quished, And Christ is Lord in - deed.
From vic - t'ry un - to vic - t'ry His ar - my shall He lead.

D. S. Till   *Fine.*   *D. S.*

2 Stand up, stand up for Jesus,
   The trumpet call obey;
Forth to the mighty conflict,
   In this His glorious day:
"Ye that are men, now serve Him,"
   Against unnumbered foes;
Your courage rise with danger,
   And strength to strength oppose.

3 Stand up, stand up for Jesus,
   Stand in His strength alone;
The arm of flesh will fail you,
   Ye dare not trust your own:

Put on the gospel armor,
   Each piece put on with prayer:
Where duty calls, or danger,
   Be never wanting there.

4 Stand up, stand up for Jesus.
   The strife will not be long;
This day the noise of battle,
   The next the victor's song:
To him that overcometh,
   A crown of life shall be;
He with the King of glory
   Shall reign eternally.

Christ, the Lord is risen Today Concluded.

No. 146. **See the Conqueror.**
Easter.

CHRISTOPHER WORDSWORTH.   CHAS. EDW. PRIOR.

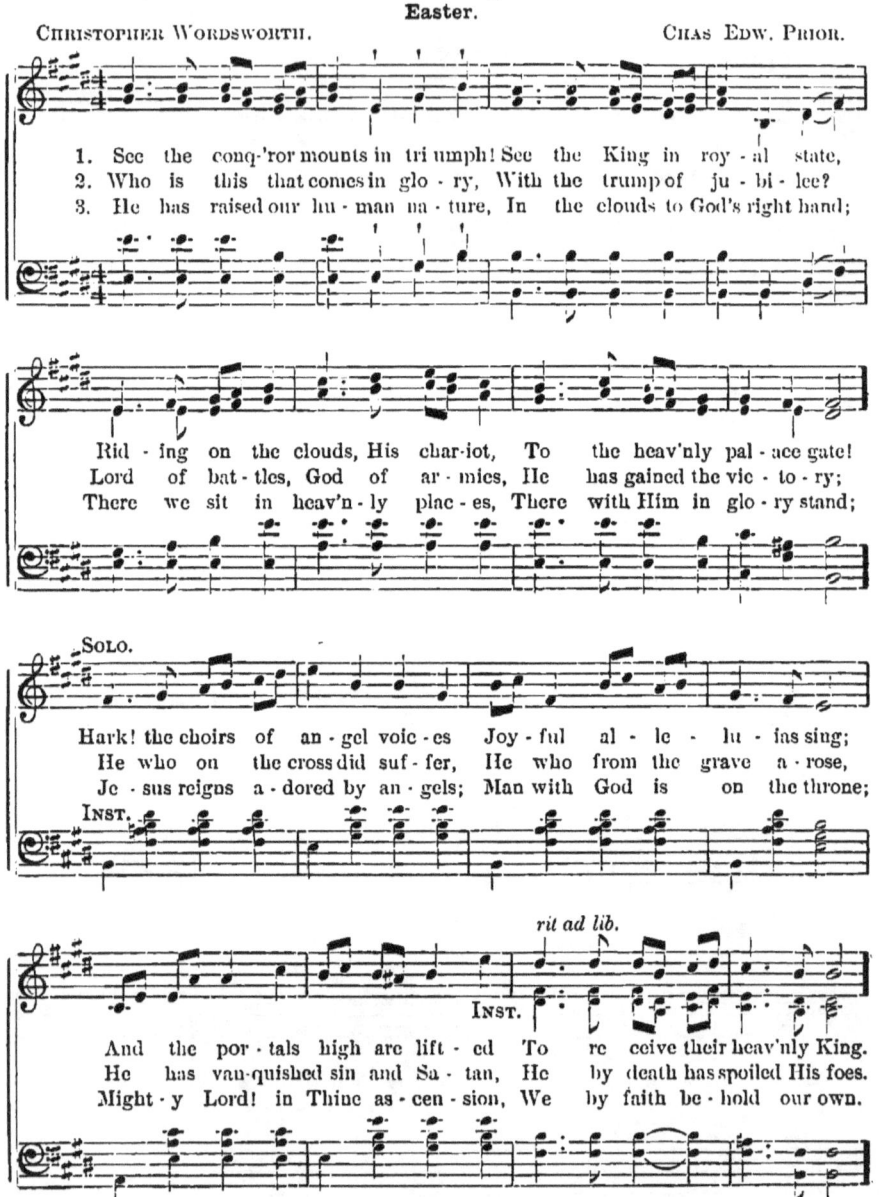

1. See the conq-'ror mounts in triumph! See the King in roy-al state,
2. Who is this that comes in glo-ry, With the trump of ju-bi-lee?
3. He has raised our hu-man na-ture, In the clouds to God's right hand;

Rid - ing on the clouds, His char-iot, To the heav'nly pal-ace gate!
Lord of bat - tles, God of ar - mies, He has gained the vic - to - ry;
There we sit in heav'n-ly plac - es, There with Him in glo - ry stand;

SOLO.

Hark! the choirs of an - gel voic - es Joy - ful al - le - lu - ias sing;
He who on the cross did suf - fer, He who from the grave a - rose,
Je - sus reigns a - dored by an - gels; Man with God is on the throne;

INST.

rit ad lib.

INST.

And the por - tals high are lift - ed To re - ceive their heav'nly King.
He has van-quished sin and Sa - tan, He by death has spoiled His foes.
Might - y Lord! in Thine as - cen - sion, We by faith be - hold our own.

By per. of Oliver Ditson Co., owner of copyright.

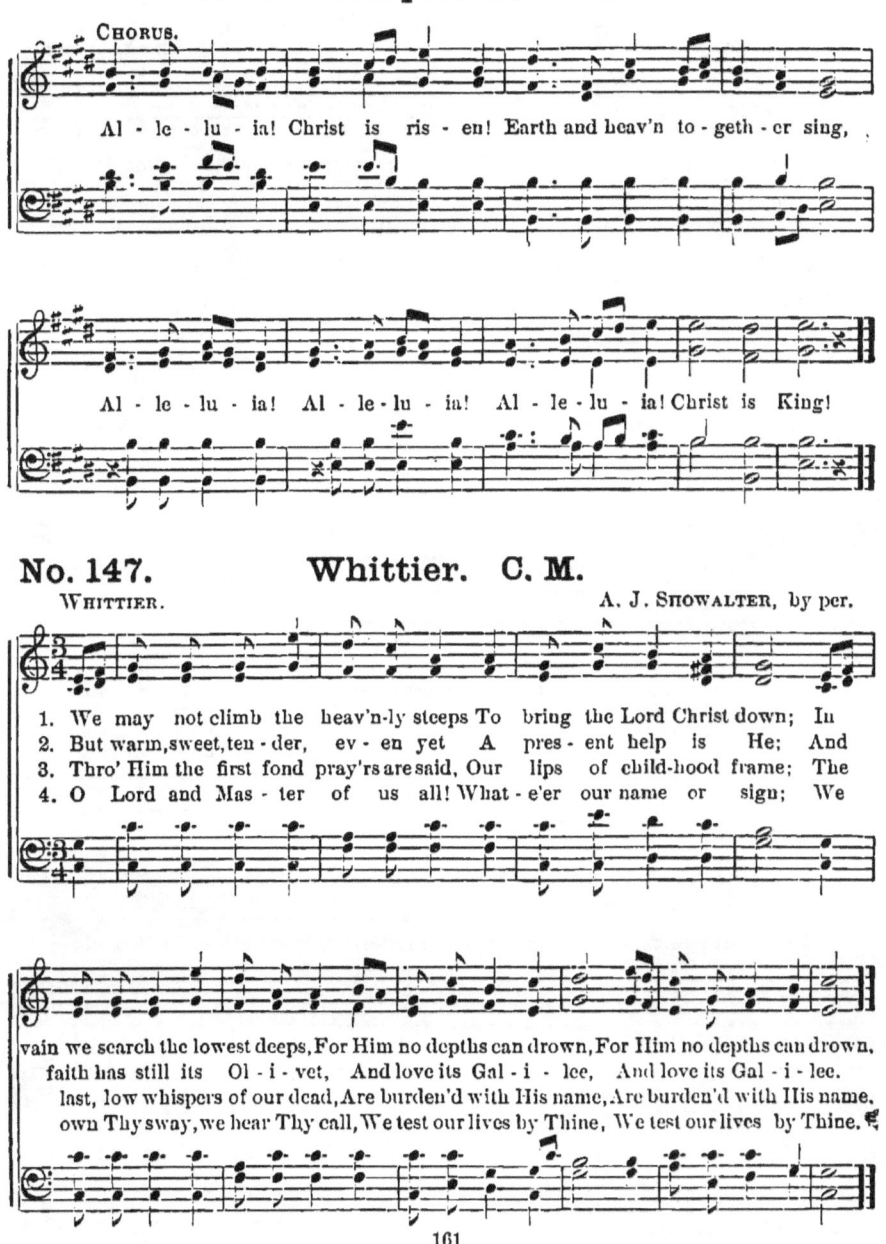

No. 149. The First Glad Song.

Mrs. E. W. Chapman.   Chas. Edw. Prior, by per.

1. Oh, pil-grims a-long life's jour-ney, The wea-ri-ness now is ours;
2. To-day we can on-ly won-der What scenes will await us there;
3. Oh, what will it be to gath-er, Be-neath the bright Jasper dome;
4. To wan-der in fade-less gar-dens, To lave in the crys-tal stream;

But o-ver the bound-less des-ert, For us the per-en-nial flow'rs.
What beau-ties be-fore us o-pen, When en-t'ring that land so fair.
To walk thro' the shin-ing cit-y, And know that it is our home.
To stand by the tide-less riv-er, Where tow'rs of the cit-y gleam.

CHORUS.

Oh, how can we tell the rap-ture, The joy of the first glad song;

When we shall the pearl gate en-ter, And see the bright an-gel throng.

Copyright, by Wharton & Barron.
163

No. 152. Retreat. L. M.

Dr. T. Hastings, 1822.

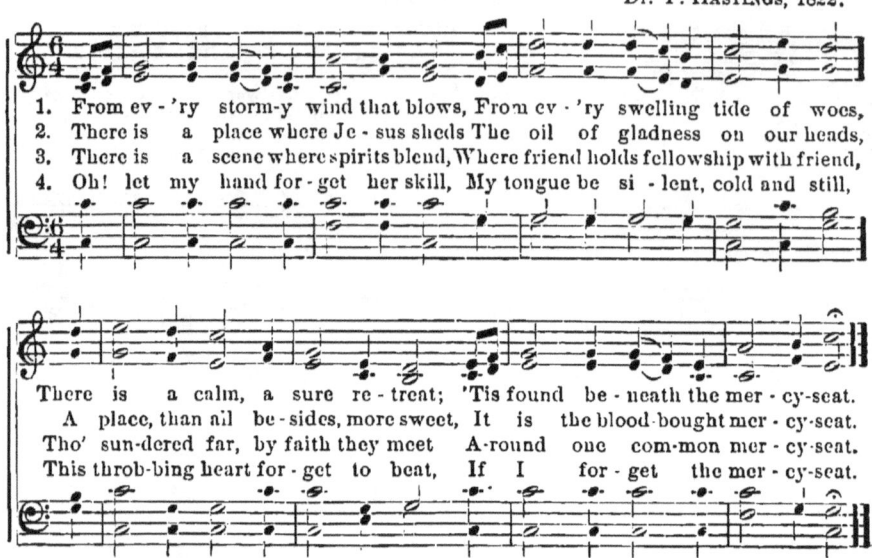

1. From ev-'ry storm-y wind that blows, From ev-'ry swelling tide of woes,
   There is a calm, a sure re-treat; 'Tis found be-neath the mer-cy-seat.
2. There is a place where Je-sus sheds The oil of gladness on our heads,
   A place, than all be-sides, more sweet, It is the blood-bought mer-cy-seat.
3. There is a scene where spirits blend, Where friend holds fellowship with friend,
   Tho' sun-dered far, by faith they meet A-round one com-mon mer-cy-seat.
4. Oh! let my hand for-get her skill, My tongue be si-lent, cold and still,
   This throb-bing heart for-get to beat, If I for-get the mer-cy-seat.

No. 153.

1 Jesus! and shall it ever be,
  A mortal man ashamed of Thee!
  Ashamed of Thee, whom angels praise,
  Whose glories shine thro' endless days!

2 Ashamed of Jesus, that dear Friend,
  On whom my hopes of heav'n depend!
  No, when I blush, be this my shame,
  That I no more revere His name.

3 Ashamed of Jesus! yes, I may,
  When I've no guilt to wash away,
  No tears to wipe, no good to crave,
  No fears to quell, no soul to save.

No. 154.

1 Say, sinner! hath a voice within,
  Oft whispered to thy secret soul,
  Urged thee to leave the ways of sin,
  And yield thy heart to God's control?

2 Sinner, it was a heavenly voice,—
  It was the Spirit's gracious call;
  It bade thee make the better choice,
  And haste to seek in Christ thine all.

3 Spurn not the call to life and light;
  Regard in time the warning, kind;
  That call thou mayst not always slight,
  And yet the gate of mercy find.

No. 155.

1 Awake, my soul, in joyful lays,
  And sing thy great Redeemer's praise;
  He justly claims a song from thee,
  His loving kindness, oh, how free!

2 He saw me ruined in the fall,
  Yet loved me notwithstanding all;
  He saved me from my lost estate,
  His loving kindness, oh, how great!

3 Often I feel my sinful heart
  Prone from my Saviour to depart;
  But, though I oft have Him forgot,
  His loving kindness changes not.

4 Soon shall I pass the gloomy vale,
  Soon all my mortal powers must fail;
  Oh, may my last, expiring breath
  His loving kindness sing in death

No. 156.

1 O Thou, to whose all-searching sight
  The darkness shineth as the light,
  Search, prove my heart, it pants for Thee;
  Oh, burst these bonds and set it free!

2 Wash out its stains, refine its dross,
  Nail my affections to the cross;
  Hallow each thought, let all within
  Be clean as Thou, my Lord, art clean.

No. 157. Hursley. L. M.

Arr. from F. J. Haydn.

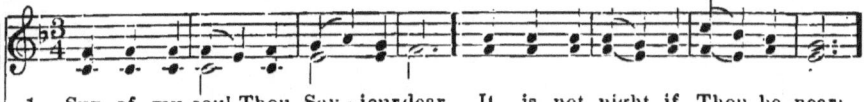
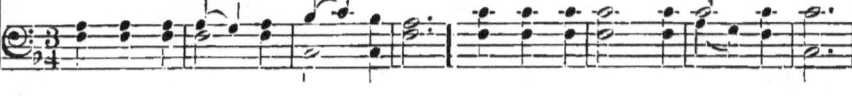

1. Sun of my soul, Thou Saviour dear, It is not night if Thou be near;
2. When the soft dews of kindly sleep, My wearied eyelids gently steep,
3. Abide with me from morn till eve, For without Thee I cannot live;
4. If some poor wand'ring child of Thine Have spurned today the voice divine,
5. Come near and bless us when we wake, Ere thro' the world our way we take,

Oh, may no earth-born cloud arise, To hide Thee from Thy servant's eyes.
Be my last tho't, how sweet to rest For ever on my Saviour's breast.
Abide with me when death is nigh, For without Thee I dare not die.
Now, Lord, the gracious work begin, Let Him no more lie down in sin.
Till in the ocean of Thy love, We lose ourselves in heav'n above.

No. 158.

1 Just as I am, without one plea,
  But that Thy blood was shed for me,
  And that Thou bid'st me come to Thee,
  O Lamb of God! I come, I come!

2 Just as I am, and waiting not
  To rid my soul of one dark blot,
  To Thee, whose blood can cleanse each spot
  O Lamb of God! I come, I come!

3 Just as I am; Thou wilt receive,
  Wilt welcome, pardon, cleanse, relieve;
  Because Thy promise I believe,
  O Lamb of God! I come, I come!

No. 159.

1 O that my load of sin were gone;
  O that I could at last submit
  At Jesus' feet to lay it down—
  To lay my soul at Jesus' feet.

2 Rest for my soul I long to find;
  Saviour of all, if mine Thou art,
  Give me Thy meek and lowly mind,
  And stamp Thine image on my heart.

3 Break off the yoke of inbred sin,
  And fully set my spirit free;
  I cannot rest till pure within,—
  Till I am wholly lost in Thee.

No. 160.

1 When I survey the wondrous cross
  On which the Prince of glory died,
  My richest gain I count but loss,
  And pour contempt on all my pride.

2 See, from His head, His hands, His feet,
  Sorrow and love flow mingled down;
  Did e'er such love and sorrow meet,
  Or thorns compose so rich a crown?

3 Were the whole realm of nature mine,
  That were a present far too small;
  Love so amazing, so divine,
  Demands my soul, my life, my all!

No. 161.

1 Lord, I am Thine, entirely Thine,
  Purchased and saved by blood divine;
  With full consent Thine I would be,
  And own Thy sov'reign right in me.

2 Thine would I live, Thine would I die;
  Be Thine through all eternity;
  The vow is past, beyond repeal,
  And now I set the solemn seal.

3 Here, at that cross where flows the blood
  That bought my guilty soul for God,
  Thee, my new Master, now I call,
  And consecrate to Thee my all.

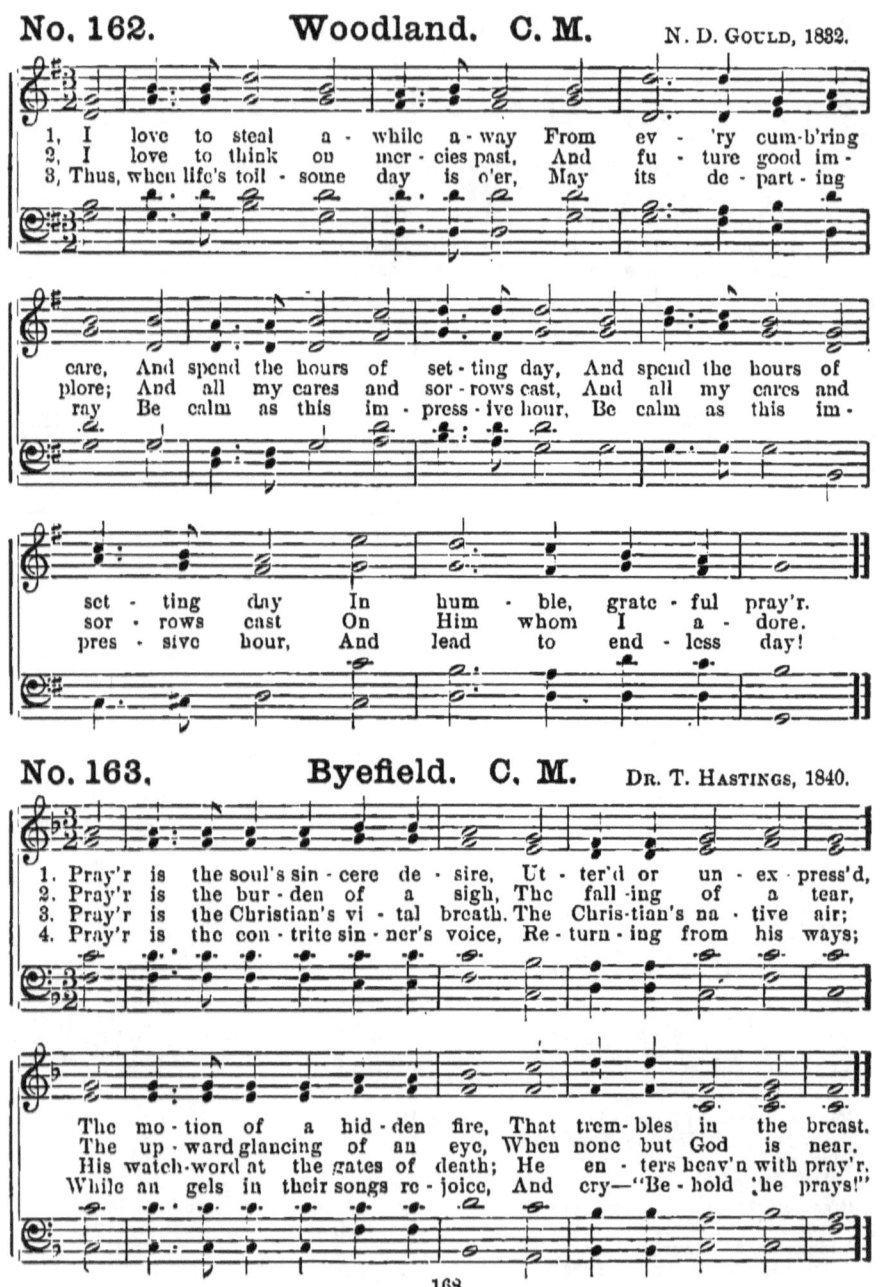

No. 164. Naomi. C. M.

Dr. Lowell Mason, 1836.

1. Father, whate'er of earthly bliss Thy sov-'reign will de-nies,
2. Give me a calm, a thankful heart, From ev-'ry murmur free;
3. Let the sweet hope that Thou art mine, My life and death at-tend;

Ac-cept-ed at Thy throne of grace, Let this pe-ti-tion rise:
The bless-ings of Thy grace im-part, And make me live to Thee
Thy pres-ence thro' my jour-ney shine, And crown my jour-ney's end.

No. 165. Avon. C. M.

H. Wilson.

1. Dear Father, to Thy mer-cy-seat My soul for shel-ter flies;
2. My cheer-ful hope can nev-er die, If Thou, my God, art near;
3. Oh, nev-er let my soul re-move From this di-vine re-treat!

'Tis here I find a safe re-treat When storms and tem-pests rise.
Thy grace can raise my com-forts high, And ban-ish ev-'ry fear.
Still let me trust Thy pow'r and love, And dwell be-neath Thy feet.

No. 166. EVAN. C. M.
W. H. HAVERGAL.

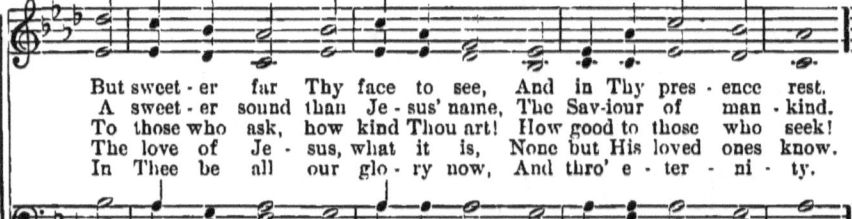

1. Je-sus, the ver-y thought of Thee, With sweet-ness fills the breast;
2. No voice can sing, no heart can frame, Nor can the mem-'ry find
3. O Hope of ev-'ry con-trite heart, O joy of all the meek,
4. But what to those who find? Ah this Nor tongue nor pen can show!
5. Je-sus, our on-ly joy be Thou, As Thou our prize wilt be;

But sweet-er far Thy face to see, And in Thy pres-ence rest.
A sweet-er sound than Je-sus' name, The Sav-iour of man-kind.
To those who ask, how kind Thou art! How good to those who seek!
The love of Je-sus, what it is, None but His loved ones know.
In Thee be all our glo-ry now, And thro' e-ter-ni-ty.

No. 167.

1 Come, Holy Spirit, heavenly Dove,
   With all Thy quick'ning powers;
Kindle a flame of sacred love
   In these cold hearts of ours.

2 Father, and shall we ever live
   At this poor dying rate—
Our love so faint, so cold to Thee,
   And Thine to us so great?

3 Come, Holy Spirit, heavenly Dove,
   With all Thy quick'ning powers;
Come, shed abroad a Saviour's love,
   And that shall kindle ours.

No. 168.

1 Am I a soldier of the cross,—
   A foll'wer of the Lamb,
And shall I fear to own His cause,
   Or blush to speak His name?

2 Are there no foes for me to face?
   Must I not stem the flood?
Is this vile world a friend to grace,
   To help me on to God?

3 Sure I must fight if I would reign;
   Increase my courage, Lord!
I'll bear the toil, endure the pain,
   Supported by Thy word.

No. 169.

1 Oh, for a closer walk with God,
   A calm and heavenly frame;
A light to shine upon the road
   That leads me to the Lamb

2 The dearest idol I have known,
   Whate'er that idol be,
Help me to tear it from Thy Throne,
   And worship only Thee.

3 So shall my walk be close with God,
   Calm and serene my frame;
So purer light shall mark the road
   That leads me to the Lamb.

No 170.

1 Forever here my rest shall be,
   Close to Thy bleeding side;
This all my hope, and all my plea,
   For me the Saviour died!

2 My dying Saviour, and my God,
   Fountain for guilt and sin,
Sprinkle me ever with Thy blood,
   And cleanse, and keep me clean.

3 Wash me, and make me thus Thine own;
   Wash me, and mine Thou art,
Wash me, but not my feet alone,
   My hands, my head, my heart.

No. 171. Coronation. C. M.

OLIVER HOLDEN.

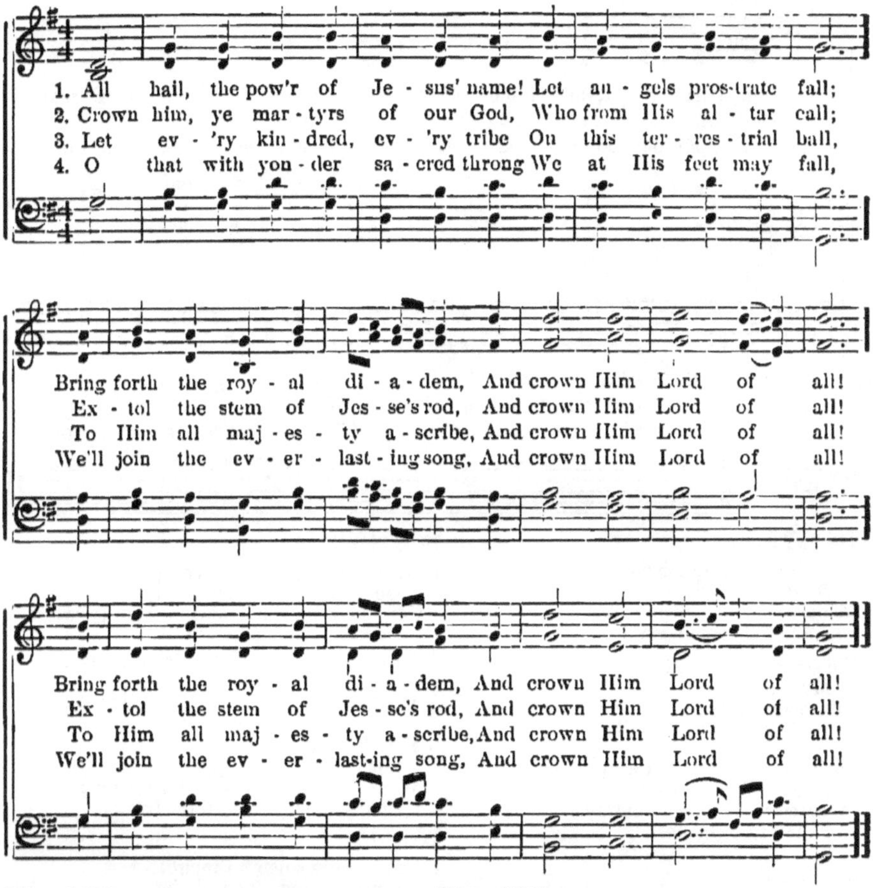
1. All hail, the pow'r of Je - sus' name! Let an - gels pros-trate fall;
2. Crown him, ye mar - tyrs of our God, Who from His al - tar call;
3. Let ev - 'ry kin - dred, ev - 'ry tribe On this ter - res - trial ball,
4. O that with yon - der sa - cred throng We at His feet may fall,
Bring forth the roy - al di - a - dem, And crown Him Lord of all!
Ex - tol the stem of Jes - se's rod, And crown Him Lord of all!
To Him all maj - es - ty a - scribe, And crown Him Lord of all!
We'll join the ev - er - last - ing song, And crown Him Lord of all!
Bring forth the roy - al di - a - dem, And crown Him Lord of all!
Ex - tol the stem of Jes - se's rod, And crown Him Lord of all!
To Him all maj - es - ty a - scribe, And crown Him Lord of all!
We'll join the ev - er - last-ing song, And crown Him Lord of all!

No. 172.

1 Salvation! oh, the joyful sound!
What pleasure to our ears;
A sov'reign balm for every wound,
A cordial for our fears.

2 Salvation! let the echo fly
The spacious world around,
While all the armies of the sky
Conspire to raise the sound.

3 Salvation! O Thou bleeding Lamb!
To Thee the praise belongs;
Salvation shall inspire our hearts,
And dwell upon our tongues.

No. 173.

1 Oh, for a thousand tongues to sing
My great Redeemer's praise!
The glories of my God and King,
The triumphs of His grace!

2 My gracious Master, and my God,
Assist me to proclaim,
To spread through all the earth abroad,
The honors of Thy name.

3 He breaks the power of canceled sin,
He sets the pris'ner free;
His blood can make the foulest clean,
His blood availed for *me*.

No. 174.   Olmutz. S. M.
GREGORIAN, 1832.

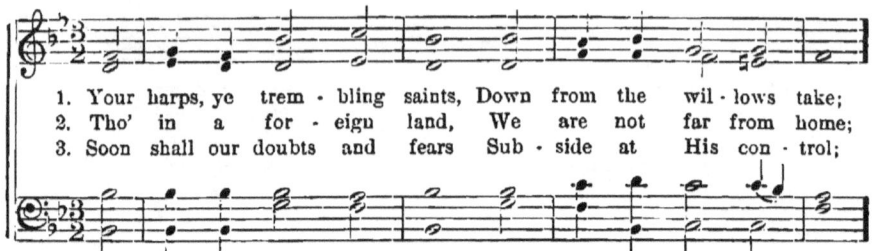

1. Your harps, ye trembling saints, Down from the willows take;
2. Tho' in a foreign land, We are not far from home;
3. Soon shall our doubts and fears Subside at His control;

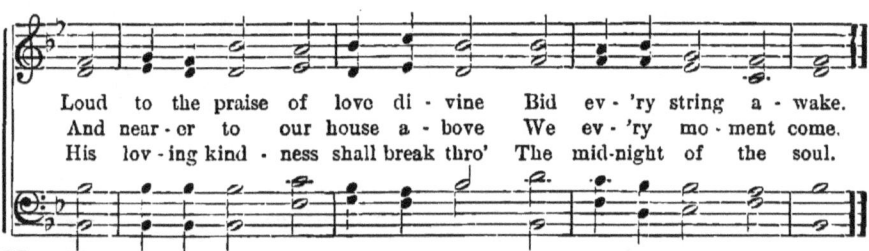

Loud to the praise of love divine Bid ev'ry string awake.
And nearer to our house above We ev'ry moment come.
His loving kindness shall break thro' The midnight of the soul.

No. 175.

1 A charge to keep I have,
   A God to glorify;
   A never-dying soul to save,
   And fit it for the sky.

2 To serve the present age,
   My calling to fulfill—
   Oh, may it all my powers engage
   To do my Master's will.

3 Help me to watch and pray,
   And on Thyself rely,
   Assured if I my trust betray,
   I shall forever die.

No. 176.

1 Behold the throne of grace;
   The promise calls us near;
   There Jesus shows a smiling face,
   And waits to answer prayer.

2 Thine image, Lord, bestow,
   Thy presence and Thy love—
   That we may serve Thee here below,
   And reign with Thee above.

3 Teach us to live by faith—
   Conform our wills to Thine;
   Let us victorious be in death,
   And then in glory shine.

No. 177.

1 Give to the winds thy fears;
   Hope, and be undismayed;
   God hears thy sighs and counts thy tears;
   God shall lift up thy head.

2 Through waves, and clouds, and storms,
   He gently clears thy way;
   Wait thou this time; so shall this night
   Soon end in joyous day.

3 Far, far above thy thought,
   His counsel shall appear,
   When fully He the work hath wrought,
   That caused thy needless fear.

No. 178.

1 One sweetly solemn thought
   Comes to me o'er and o'er;
   'Tis that I'm nearer home to-day
   Than e'er I've been before.

2 Nearer my Father's house
   Where many mansions be;
   Nearer the solemn judgment throne,
   Nearer the jasper sea.

3 Nearer the bound where life
   Shall lay its burdens down;
   Where I shall leave my ill-borne cross,
   And take my blood-bought crown.

4 Saviour, perfect my trust,
   Confirm my feeble faith,
   And teach me fearlessly to stand
   Upon the shore of death.

No. 179. St. Thomas. S. M.

A. WILLIAMS.

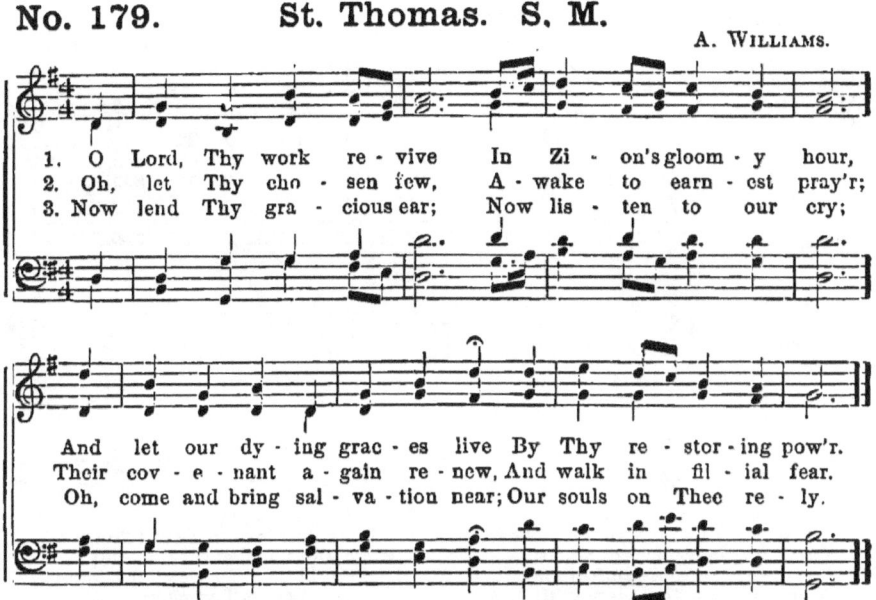

1. O Lord, Thy work revive In Zion's gloomy hour, And let our dying graces live By Thy restoring pow'r.
2. Oh, let Thy chosen few, Awake to earnest pray'r; Their covenant again renew, And walk in filial fear.
3. Now lend Thy gracious ear; Now listen to our cry; Oh, come and bring salvation near; Our souls on Thee rely.

No. 180.

1 Sow in the morn thy seed;
   At eve hold not thy hand;
To doubt and fear give thou no heed,
   Broadcast it o'er the land.

2 Thou know'st not which shall thrive,
   The late or early sown;
Grace keeps the perfect germ alive,
   When and wherever strewn.

3 Thou canst not toil in vain;
   Cold, heat, and moist and dry,
Shall foster and mature the grain
   For garners in the sky.

No. 181.

1 My soul, be on thy guard,
   Ten thousand foes arise;
The hosts of sin are pressing hard
   To draw thee from the skies.

2 Oh, watch, and fight, and pray!
   The battle ne'er give o'er;
Renew it boldly every day,
   And help Divine implore.

3 Ne'er think the victory won,
   Nor lay thine armor down;
The work of faith will not be done,
   Till thou obtain the crown.

No. 182.

1 I love Thy kingdom, Lord,
   The house of Thine abode—
The Church our blest Redeemer saved
   With His own precious blood.

2 I love Thy Church, O God!
   Her walls before Thee stand
Dear as the apple of Thine eye,
   And graven on Thy hand.

3 For her my tears shall fall;
   For her my prayers ascend;
To her my cares and toils be given,
   Till toils and cares shall end.

No. 183.

1 To Thee I lift my soul;
   O Lord, I trust in Thee!
My God, let me not be ashamed,
   Nor foes triumph o'er me.

2 Let none that wait on Thee
   Be put to shame at all;
But those that without cause transgress,
   Let shame upon them fall.

3 Show me Thy ways, O Lord!
   Thy paths, oh, teach Thou me!
And do Thou lead me in Thy truth,
   Therein my Teacher be.

No. 184.   Martyn. 7s.

S. B. Marsh, 1836.

2 Other refuge have I none;
   Hangs my helpless soul on Thee;
   Leave, ah, leave me not alone!
   Still support and comfort me;
   All my trust on Thee is stay'd;
   All my help from Thee I bring;
   Cover my defenceless head
   With the shadow of Thy wing.

3 Thou, O Christ, art all I want,
   Boundless love in Thee I find,
   Raise the fallen, cheer the faint,
   Heal the sick, and lead the blind
   Just and holy is Thy name,
   I am all unrighteousness;
   Vile and full of sin I am—
   Thou art full of truth and grace.

No. 185.   Toplady. 7s.

Dr. T. Hastings.

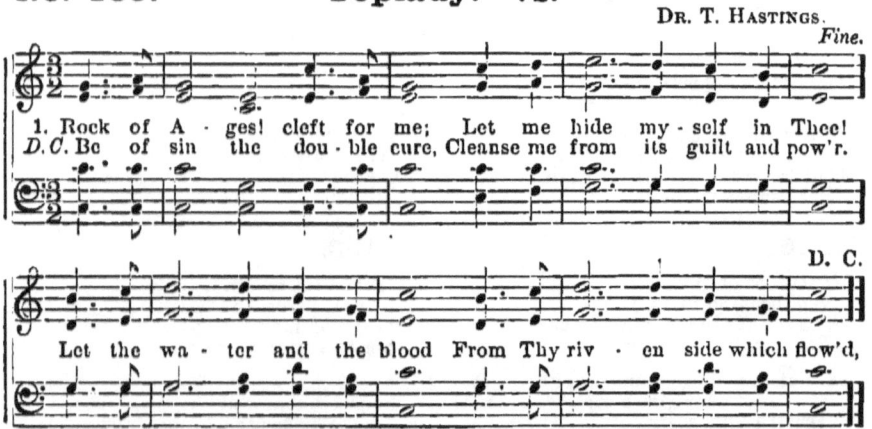

2 Could my zeal no respite know,
   Could my tears forever flow—
   All for sin could not atone:
   Thou must save, and Thou alone!
   Nothing in my hand I bring;
   Simply to Thy cross I cling.

3 While I draw this fleeting breath,
   When my eyelids close in death,
   When I soar to worlds unknown,
   See Thee on Thy judgment throne,
   Rock of Ages! cleft for me,
   Let me hide myself in Thee!

INDEX.

Title in SMALL CAPS, First Line Roman Letters.

Title / First Line	No.
A brave, loyal army of Soldiers.	83
A charge to keep I Have.	175
A CUP OF WATER.	76
Alas! and did my Saviour Bleed.	123
ALL HAIL, MIGHTY SAVIOUR.	143
All hail the power of Jesus' Name.	171
ALL THINGS ARE YOURS.	95
Am I a soldier of the Cross.	168
AN ENDLESS ALLELUIA.	51
Are you tenting toward the Highlands.	34
Are you walking with the Saviour.	59
AT THE BLEST NATIVITY.	139
At the fading of the silent Night.	84
A VOICE FROM HEAVEN.	116
AVON.	163
Away, my soul, in joyful Lays.	155
BEAUTIFUL BETHLEHEM.	17
Behold the throne of Grace.	175
BE OF GOOD CHEER.	14
Blessed Jesus, guide my Feet.	42
Blest were the Lord's Disciples.	122
Brightest flowers and lilies Sweet.	58
Bright flower we bring, the cross to Deck.	69
BYEFIELD.	163
CALLIE.	9
CALLING AGAIN.	55
Care-worn traveler on life's Ocean.	96
CHRIST, THE LORD, IS RISEN TO-DAY.	145
CLINGING TO THE CROSS.	79
Close beside the throne of Grace.	52
Come, Holy Spirit, Heavenly Dove.	167
COME TO THE FOUNTAIN.	60
COME TO THE SAVIOUR.	26
COME UNTO ME.	50–91
Come unto me, ye Weary.	29
Come where the Master is Calling.	65
COME, YE WEARY.	29
CORONATION.	171
CRESSEY.	123
DANIEL, THE CAPTIVE.	115
Dear Father, to Thy mercy Seat.	165
DEAR SAVIOUR, BEND THINE EAR.	7
Down at the feet of the Lowly.	27
ENDURE TO THE END.	36
EVAN.	166
EVER WILL I PRAY.	125
Father, in the Morning.	125
Father, whate'er of earthly Bliss.	164
Far o'er the mountain the Shepherd.	55
Forever here my rest shall Be.	170
FOR THE MASTER'S SAKE.	126
Fresh from the springs Eternal.	28
From every stormy wind that Blows.	152
GATHERING HOMEWARD.	101
GATHER JEWELS.	102
Give to the winds thy Fears.	177
GOLDEN GATES.	99
GOODWIN.	144
GRANDLY MARCHING ON.	67
GUIDE AND GUARD.	42
Hark! a voice from Heaven.	116
Hark, hark the song, our Souls.	109
HAIL THE MIGHTY CONQUEROR.	58
HAPPY CHILDREN'S DAY.	68
HEAR HIS EARNEST PLEA.	52
Hear how the angels Sing.	140
Hear the Master's loving Voice.	120
Hear the Merry Christmas Bells.	142
Hear the Saviour's voice To-day.	91
HE CARES FOR YOU.	8
HE THAT BELIEVETH.	15
HEART AND VOICE.	84
HELP ME OR I DIE.	88
HEAVEN SHALL RING.	19
HO! EVERY ONE THAT THINKETH.	118
HOMEWARD BOUND.	74
HOW SHALL I LIVE.	31
How sweet is the Thought.	24
HURSLEY.	157
I had wandered far from Home.	134
I love Thy Kingdom, Lord.	182
I love to steal awhile Away.	162
I long for household voices Gone.	9
I KNOW, AND I AM TRUSTING.	80
I know of a stream that Floweth.	80
I know that my Redeemer Liveth.	81
I may not have silver nor Gold.	107
I SHALL BE SATISFIED.	20
I SHALL BE WHITER THAN SNOW.	92
I WILL FOLLOW JESUS.	105
I WILL GIVE YOU REST.	108
I will live for my Redeemer.	41
I WILL TRUST MY DEAR REDEEMER.	41
If beset by doubts and Fears.	23
If the sweet peace of Jesus is Filling.	73
IN HIS NAME.	75
In the cross of Christ I Glory.	79
IN THE LAND OF THE FOREVER.	35
In the fields of life's great Harvest.	39
IN THE SHADOW OF THE CROSS.	90
IN THE SHADOW OF THE ROCK.	87
Jesus! and shall it ever Be.	153
JESUS IS CALLING.	38
JESUS IS OUR SHEPHERD.	70
JESUS IS PRECIOUS.	119
Jesus is tenderly Calling.	38
JESUS, I COME TO THEE.	98
Jesus, let the Holy Spirit.	12
Jesus, lover of my Soul.	184
Jesus, Saviour, meek and Lowly.	121
JESUS SHALL REIGN.	119
JESUS, TENDER SHEPHERD.	64
Jesus, the very thought of Thee.	168
JOYFULLY MARCHING ONWARD.	4
Just as I am, without one Plea.	158
KEEP FAITHFUL OUR HEARTS.	130
Knocking at the Door.	133
LET ALL THE CHILDREN SING.	72
Let us work in cheerful Way.	126
LIFE, ETERNAL LIFE.	114
LIVING FOR JESUS.	47
Lord, I am Thine, entirely Thine.	161
LOVE OF JESUS.	77
LOYAL TO JESUS.	54
Marching on, with Christ.	67
MARTYN.	184
MY OWN DEAR FATHERLAND.	129
MY REDEEMER LIVETH.	81
MY SAVIOUR DEAR, I COME.	18
My soul be on thy Guard.	181
NAOMI.	164
NEARING THE BETTER LAND.	96
NO NIGHT THERE.	62
No night within that glorious Home.	62
Not will of mine.	32
Of a King we are the Daughters.	75
O blessed hope Immortal.	5
O COME, LET US WORSHIP.	97
O, I am so happy in Jesus.	15
O Lord, thy work Revive.	179
O LOOK NOT BACK.	56
O that my load of sin were Gone.	159
O, tell me not to pause, vain World.	114
O, the day of life is Closing.	130

175

INDEX.—Continued.

Title	Page
O those to whose all-searching Sight	156
O thou tender loving Saviour	88
O weary soul, with sin Distressed	50
O what can Little hands Do	86
Oh, for a closer walk with God	169
Oh, for a thousand tongues to Sing	173
Oh, hear the angel's Song	140
Oh, pilgrims along life's Journey	149
Oh, what shall we bring to the Master	89
O'er the hills and through the Dells	145
Olmutz	174
Once more with Gladness	141
Once the Saviour took the Children	85
One sweetly Solemn Thought	178
Only a cup of Water	78
On the cross at Calvary	120
On the Jerico Road	23
Onward, Christian Soldiers	151
Our Father who art in Heaven	135
Our trusting hearts Rejoice	5
Over the hilltops the Morning	10
Passing thro' this world of Sorrow	76
Praise the Lord of Heaven	93
Praise ye the Lord	53
Praises to our Saviour King	10
Prayer is the soul's sincere Desire	163
Precious blood of Jesus	110
Precious is the Saviour's Promise	8
Press toward the Prize	128
Remember Me	44
Rest, dearest brother, thy Journey	48
Rest of the Weary	13
Rest, weary One	48
Retreat	152
Ring out each chiming Bell	141
Ring the Bells	136
Rock of Ages! cleft for Me	185
Sabbath Morn has Come	71
Salvation! oh, the joyful Sound	172
Saviour King, I would Sing	100
Say not, my soul, 'tis Night	137
Say, sinner, hath a voice Within	154
Scatter the Sunbeams	113
See the Conqueror	146
See the star in yonder Heavens	138
Shine around Me	12
Shining for Jesus	131
Shout for Joy	148
Sing alleluia forth in duteous Praise	51
Sing Aloud	69
Sing me a song of the Heavenly Land	63
Songs of the Kingdom we will Sing	2
Sparkling and Bright	1-2
Speak of it Now	73
Sow in the morn the Seed	180
Stand by the Home	132
Stand up for Jesus	144
Star and Song	138
Striving to do my Master's Will	47
St. Gertrude	151
St. Thomas	179
Such as I have will I Bring	107
Suffer the Children	85
Sun of my soul, then Saviour Dear	157
Sweet are the Promises	94
Sweet songs are heard in the Woodland	72
Sweet thoughts of God	24
Swing open the portals of Glory	11
Teach us to Pray	104
Tenting toward the Highlands	34
The army of Jesus	83
The bells of Heaven are Ringing	27
The bells of the beautiful City	11
The birthday of our King	142
The children's Band	46
The fields appear in Beauty	68
The first glad Song	149
The glad over There	45
The harvest Time	65
The Heavenly Land	63
The hours of day are Over	106
The life of Jesus	6
The living Stream	28
The Lord is the theme of my Song	25
The Lord's Prayer	135
The mountain, hill and Valley	95
The nations honor Heroes	6
The new Morning	10
The order went forth to the Soldiers	115
The Saviour hath called Thee	111
The Saviour was Sleeping	143
The vessel is out in the Tempest	14
The world is very Beautiful	105
Thanks be to God	3
There is a bright home just Beyond	129
There's a mansion o'er the River	35
There's a nation to be Stirred	136
There's a place above all Others	90
There's a prize in the Kingdom	128
Though fierce the Temptation	36
Through the blood of Jesus	43
Throw open the Gates	61
The grace, O my Saviour	92
Thy will be Done	32
'Tis a battle for the Home	132
'Tis not for pleasure duty Calls	112
'Tis sweet to Know	127
'Tis the love of Jesus	77
Toiling together with God	150
Toplady	185
To thee I lift my Soul	183
Trust and Obey	21
Trusting every Day	25
Wait a little, you may See	33
Waiting for Day	39
Waiting on the Shore	103
Walking the Sea	122
Walking with the Saviour	59
Weary of Sin	121
We came a merry Band	82
We came with songs of Gladness	82
We may not climb the Heavenly	147
We met like the early Disciples	130
We praise the Redeemer	40
We're a band of little Children	46
We're shining for Jesus	131
We shall reach our home some Day	43
We shall Rest	57
What can little hands Do	86
What shall we Bring	89
When from out the shining Gateway	139
When I shall walk in That	20
When I survey the wondrous Cross	160
When lost in the Darkness	30
When storms around are Sweeping	44
When the pearly gates Unfold	45
When the shadows deep are Falling	108
When we walk with the Lord	21
Where He leads I'll Follow	94
Where they never say Farewell	124
Whittier	147
Who at my door is Standing	133
Who is on the Lord's Side	37
Who is ready for the Harvest	39
Who is this that Cometh	16
Who will Win	112
Why not trust in Him Now	111
Why the Saviour loves me So	134
Wilt there be made Whole	117
Woodland	162
Work for the Master	66
Working for Jesus	22
Yonder are many Mansions	49
Your harps, ye trembling Saints	174

www.ingramcontent.com/pod-product-compliance
Lightning Source LLC
Chambersburg PA
CBHW020257170426
43202CB00008B/411